INTUITION

INTUITION

Knowing Beyond Logic

osho

·

*insights for a
new way of living*

St. Martin's Griffin ♞ New York

www.stmartins.com

Editing and compilation by Leela Itzler

Haiku poem by Bashō, translated by Thomas Byron, is from *The Dhammapada: The Sayings of the Buddha: A New Rendering*, published by Alfred A. Knopf, 1976. Reprinted by permission.

Library of Congress Cataloging-in-Publication Data

Osho, 1931–1990.
    Intuition : knowing beyond logic / Osho.—1st ed.
      p.   cm.—(Insights for a new way of living)
    ISBN 0-312-27567-6
    1. Intuition. I. Title.

BP605.R34 I583 2001
299'.93—dc21   2001041961

10 9 8 7 6 5

Contents

Foreword

~~~

Intuition cannot be explained scientifically because the very phenomenon is unscientific and irrational. The very phenomenon of intuition is irrational. In language it looks okay to ask, "Can intuition be explained?" But it means, "Can intuition be reduced to intellect?" And intuition is something beyond the intellect, something not of the intellect, something coming from some place where intellect is totally unaware. So the intellect can *feel* it, but it cannot explain it.

The leap of intuition can be felt because there is a gap. Intuition can be felt by the intellect—it can be noted that something has happened—but it cannot be explained, because explanation needs causality. Explanation means to answer the question from where does it come, why does it come, what is the cause. And it comes from somewhere else, not from the intellect itself—so there is no intellectual cause. There is no reason, no link, no continuity within the intellect.

Intuition is a different realm of happening that is not related to the intellect at all, although it can penetrate the intellect. It must be understood that a higher reality can penetrate a lower reality, but the lower cannot penetrate the higher. So intuition can penetrate intellect because it is higher, but intellect cannot penetrate intuition because it is lower.

It is just like your mind can penetrate your body, but your body cannot penetrate the mind. Your being can penetrate the mind, but the mind cannot penetrate the being. That is why, if you are going into the being, you have to separate yourself from body and mind both. They cannot penetrate a higher phenomenon.

As you go into a higher reality, the lower world of happenings has to be dropped. There is no explanation of the higher in the lower because the very terms of explanation don't exist there; they are meaningless. But the intellect can feel the gap, it can know the gap. It can come to feel that "something has happened that is beyond me." If even this much can be done, the intellect has done much.

But intellect can also reject what has happened. That is what is meant by having faith or not having faith. If you feel that what cannot be explained by the intellect does not exist, then you are a "nonbeliever." Then you will continue in this lower existence of the intellect, tethered to it. Then you disallow mystery, then you disallow intuition to speak to you.

> If you feel that what cannot be explained by the intellect does not exist, then you are a "nonbeliever." Then you disallow mystery, then you disallow intuition to speak to you.

This is what a rationalist is. The rationalist will not even see that something from the beyond has come. If you are rationally trained, you will not allow the higher; you will deny it, you will say, "It cannot be. It must be my imagination; it must be my dream. Unless I can prove it rationally, I will not accept it." A rational mind becomes closed, closed within the boundaries of reasoning, and intuition cannot penetrate.

But you can use the intellect without being closed. Then you can use reason as an instrument, and you remain open. You are receptive to the higher; if something comes, you are receptive. Then you can use your intellect as a help. It notes that "something has happened that is beyond me." It can help you to understand this gap.

Beyond that, intellect can be used for expression—not for explanation, for expression. A buddha does not "explain" anything. He is expressive, but nonexplanatory. All the Upanishads are expressive without any explanations. They say, "This is such, this is so; this is what is happening. If you want, come in. Do not stand outside; no explanation is possible from the inside to the outside. So come in—become an insider."

Even if you come inside, things will not be explained to you; you will come to know and feel them. Intellect can try to understand, but it is bound to be a failure. The higher cannot be reduced to the lower.

INTUITION TRAVELS WITHOUT ANY VEHICLE—that is why it is a jump; that is why it is a leap. It is a jump from one point to another point, with no interconnection between the two. If I come to you step-by-step, it is not a jump. Only if I come to you without any steps is it a jump. And a *real* jump is even deeper. It means that something exists on point A, and then it exists on point B, and between the two there is no existence. That is a real jump.

Intuition is a jump—it is not something that comes to you in steps. It is something happening to you, not coming to you—something happening to you without any causality anywhere, without any source anywhere. This sudden happening means intuition. If it were not sudden, not completely discontinuous with what went before, then reason would discover the path. It would take time, but it could be done. Reason would be capable of knowing and understanding and controlling it. Then any day an instrument could be developed, just like radio or TV, in which intuitions could be received.

If intuition came through rays or waves, then we could make an instrument to receive them. But no instrument can pick up intuition because it is not a wave phenomenon. It is not a phenomenon at all; it is just a leap from nothing to being.

Intuition means just that—that's why reason denies it. Reason denies it because reason is incapable of encountering it. Reason can only encounter phenomena that can be divided into cause and effect.

According to reason there are two realms of existence, the known and the unknown. And the unknown means that which is not yet known but will someday be known. But mysticism says that there are three realms: the known, the unknown, and the unknowable. By the unknowable, the mystic means that which can never be known.

Intellect is involved with the known and the unknown, not with the unknowable. And intuition works with the unknowable, with that which cannot be known. It is not just a question of time before it will be known—unknowability is its intrinsic quality. It is not that your instruments are not fine enough or your logic not up-to-date, or your mathematics primitive—that is not the question. The intrinsic quality of the unknowable is unknowability; it will always exist as the unknowable.

This is the realm of intuition.

When something from the unknowable comes to be known, it is a jump—there is no link, there is no passage, there is no going from one point to another point. But it seems inconceivable, so when I say you can feel it but you cannot understand it, when I say such things, I know very well that I am uttering nonsense. "Nonsense" only means that which cannot be understood by our senses. And mind is a sense, the most subtle.

Intuition is possible *because the unknowable is there*. Science denies the existence of the divine because it says, "There is only one division: the known and the unknown. If there is any God, we will discover him through laboratory methods. If he exists, science will discover him."

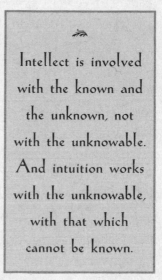

Intellect is involved with the known and the unknown, not with the unknowable. And intuition works with the unknowable, with that which cannot be known.

The mystic, on the other hand, says, "Whatever you do, something in the very foundation of existence will remain unknowable—a mystery." And if the mystics are not right, then I think that science is going to destroy the whole meaning of life. If there is no mystery, the whole meaning of life is destroyed and the whole beauty is destroyed.

The unknowable is the beauty, the meaning, the aspiration, the goal. Because of the unknowable, life means something. When

> Because of the unknowable, life means something. When everything is known, then everything is flat. You will be fed up, bored.

everything is known, then everything is flat. You will be fed up, bored.

The unknowable is the secret; it is life itself.

I will say this:

Reason is an effort to know the unknown, and intuition is the happening of the unknowable. To penetrate the unknowable is possible but to explain it is not.

The feeling is possible; the explanation is not. The more you try to explain it, the more closed you will become, so do not try. Let reason work in its own field, but remember continuously that there are deeper realms. There are deeper reasons, which reason cannot understand. Higher reasons, which reason is incapable of conceiving.

Reason is an effort to know the unknown
and intuition is the happening of the unknowable.
To penetrate the unknowable is possible,
but to explain it is not.
The feeling is possible,
the explanation is not.

MAPS

When the body functions spontaneously,
that is called instinct.
When the soul functions spontaneously,
that is called intuition.
They are alike and yet
far away from each other.
Instinct is of the body—the gross;
and intuition is of the soul—the subtle.
And between the two is the mind, the expert,
which never functions spontaneously.
Mind means knowledge.
Knowledge can never be spontaneous.
Instinct is deeper than intellect and
intuition is higher than intellect.
Both are beyond the intellect, and both are good.

HEAD, HEART, AND BEING

Your individuality can be divided—just for the purpose of understanding it; otherwise there is no division. It is one single unity, whole: the head, the heart, and the being.

Intellect is the functioning of the head, instinct is the functioning of your body, and intuition is the functioning of your heart. And behind these three is your being, whose only quality is witnessing.

The head only thinks; hence it never comes to any conclusion. It is verbal, linguistic, logical, but because it has no roots in reality, thousands of years of philosophical thinking have not given us a single conclusion. Philosophy has been the greatest exercise in futility. Intellect is very clever in creating questions and then creating answers, and then out of those answers, more questions and more answers. It can make palaces of words, systems of theories, but they are all just hot air.

The body cannot rely on your intellect, because the body has to live. That's why all essential functions of the body are in the hands of instinct—for example, breathing, heartbeat, digestion of your food, circulation of the blood. A thousand and one processes are going on inside your body in which you have no part at all. And it is good that nature has given body its own wisdom. Otherwise, if your intellect were to take care of the body, life would have been impossible! Because sometimes you may forget to breathe—at least in the night, how will you breathe while you are asleep? You are already so confused just with thoughts; in this confusion, who will take care about the blood circulation, whether the right amount of oxygen is reaching your cells or not? Whether the food that you are eating is being analyzed into its basic constituents, and those basic constituents are sent where they are needed? And this whole, tremendous amount of work is done by instinct. You are not needed. You can remain in a coma; still the body will continue to work.

Nature has given all essential functions of your body to instinct, and it has left all that makes your life meaningful . . . because just to exist, just to survive, has no meaning. To give meaning to your life, existence has given intuition to your heart. Out of your intuition arises the possibility of art, of aesthetics, of love, of friendship—all kinds of creativity are intuitive.

But the marketplace does not need your intuition. It does not deal in love, in your sensibilities; it deals with solid and mundane things. For that, your intellect—which is the most superficial part—functions. Intellect is for the mundane life with others in the marketplace, in the world, to make you capable of functioning. It is mathematics, it is geography, it is history, it is chemistry—all science and all technology are created by your intellect. Your logic and your geometry are useful—but the intellect is blind. It simply goes on creating things, but it does not know whether they are being used for destruction or for creation. A nuclear war will be a war created by intellect.

Intellect has its use, but by some misfortune it has become the master of your whole being. That has created immense troubles in the world.

The master is hidden behind these three: the body, the mind, the heart. The master is hidden behind all these three—that is your being. But you never go inward; all your roads go outward,

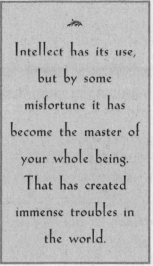

Intellect has its use, but by some misfortune it has become the master of your whole being. That has created immense troubles in the world.

all your senses go outward. All your achievements are out there in the world.

Intellect is useful in the world, and all your educational systems are techniques to avoid the heart and take your energy directly to your head. The heart can create troubles for the head—the heart knows nothing of logic. The heart has a totally different center of functioning, and that is intuition. It knows love, but love is not a commodity of any use in the world. It knows beauty, but what are you going to do with beauty in the marketplace?

> Nobody wants his or her children to become musicians or painters or dancers. Everybody wants them to be doctors, engineers, scientists, because those professions pay.

The people of the heart—the painters, the poets, the musicians, the dancers, the actors—are all irrational. They create great beauty, they are great lovers, but they are absolutely unfit in a society that is arranged by the head. Your artists are thought by your society to be almost outcast, a little bit crazy, an insane type of people. Nobody wants his or her children to become musicians or painters or dancers. Everybody wants them to be doctors, engineers, scientists, because those professions pay. Painting, poetry, dance, are dangerous, risky—you may end up just a beggar on the street, playing on your flute.

The heart has been denied—and by the way, it will be useful to remember that the denial of the heart has been the denial of the woman. And unless the heart is accepted, the woman cannot be accepted. Unless the heart has the same opportunity to grow as the head, the woman cannot have liberation. The woman is heart and the man is head. The distinction is clear.

Instinct, nature has taken in its own hands. And whenever you interfere with instinct, you create perversions. All the religions have been doing that; every religion has been interfering with the body—and the body is absolutely innocent, it has never done anything wrong. If you accept the body in its absolute naturalness, it will help you tremendously. It will help your heart, nourish your heart. It will help your intelligence to become sharper, because the nourishment for the intellect comes from the body, nourishment to the heart comes from the body. And if your head, your heart,

> I am not against anything. I am only against disharmony, and because your head is creating the most inharmonious situation, I want your head to be put in its right place. It is a servant, not a master.

and your body are all in a symphony, then to find your being is the easiest thing in the world. But because they are in conflict, your whole life goes on being wasted in that conflict, conflict between instinct and intellect and intuition.

A wise person creates a harmony between the head, the heart, and the body. In this harmony comes the revelation of the source of one's life, the very center, the soul. And that is the greatest ecstasy possible—not only to human beings but in this whole universe, nothing more is possible.

I am not against anything. I am only against disharmony, and because your head is creating the most inharmonious situation, I want your head to be put in its right place. It is a servant, not a master. As a servant it is great, helpful.

A Dublin milkman has just finished his delivery, so he parks his horse and cart outside the pub and goes in for a drink. Refreshed after an hour, he comes out to find his horse painted bright green. Angry, he strides back into the pub and demands, "Which of you just painted my horse green?"

A seven-foot Irish giant stands up and, towering over him, says, "I did. Want to do something about it?"

The milkman gives a sickly grin and says, "I just came in to tell you, the first coat is dry!"

Intellect is helpful! In some situations you will be in need of intellect—but only as a servant, not as a master.

PAST, PRESENT, AND FUTURE

You have a past and you have a present and you have a future. Instinct is what belongs to your animal past. It is very old, solid; it is the inheritance of millions of years. And when I say it is animal-like, I am not condemning it. With the word *animal* the priests of all religions have associated some condemnation—but I am simply stating a fact, with no condemnation at all. Our past was an animal past. We have passed through all kinds of animals; our evolution has been from fish up to man, passing through all the species of animals. It has been a long, long journey to arrive at mankind.

Intellect is human. It is our present. That's how we function, through intellect. All our sciences, all our businesses, all our professions, whatever is going on in the world—our politics, our religion, our philosophy—they are all based on intellect. Intellect is human.

Instinct is almost infallible because it is so old, so ripe, so mature. Your eyes are blinking—are you doing it? They go on doing it by themselves—this is instinct. Your heart is beating, your breathing is going in and out; it is not up to your intellect to look after all these essential things of life. They are in the hands of instinct because instinct is absolutely infallible. It never forgets to breathe, it never forgets anything.

The intellect is fallible because it is new, a recent arrival. It is just groping in the dark, still trying to find out what it is and where it belongs. And because it does not have roots in experience, it substitutes experience with beliefs, philosophies, ideologies. They become the focus of intellect. But they are all fallible because they are all man-made, manufactured by some clever guy. And they are not applicable in every situation. They may be right in one situation, and in another situation they may not be right. But intellect

Your heart is beating, your breathing is going in and out—all these essential things of life are in the hands of instinct because instinct is absolutely infallible. It never forgets anything.

> ❧
>
> Intellect is blind, it knows not how to deal with the new. It always brings the old answer to the new question.

is blind, it knows not how to deal with the new. It always brings the old answer to the new question.

Paddy and Sean are sitting opposite the local whorehouse in Dublin, discussing the virtues of the Catholic faith. Suddenly, Gideon Greenberg, the local rabbi, approaches the whorehouse door, looks left and right, then hurries up the stairs.

"Did you see that?" roars Paddy. "I'm glad I am a Catholic."

Ten minutes later, the Anglican priest approaches the door, looks around quickly, then dashes up the stairs.

"Another hypocrite," says Paddy, laughing. "Thank God I am a Catholic."

A few minutes later Sean nudges Paddy and says, "Hey, man, look! There is Father O'Murphy coming this way."

The two men watch in stunned silence as the Catholic priest disappears up the stairs into the whorehouse. Suddenly Paddy jumps to his feet, crosses himself, and shouts at Sean, "Where is your respect? Stand up and take off your hat! There must be a death in the house!"

Intellect lives through prejudices; it is never fair. By its very nature it cannot be, because it has no experience. Instinct is always fair and shows you exactly the natural way, the relaxed way, and the way that the universe follows. But strangely, instinct has been condemned by all religions, and intellect has been praised.

Of course, if everybody follows instinct, there is no need of any religion, no need of any God, no need of any priest. Animals don't need God and they are perfectly happy—I don't see that they are missing God. Not a single animal, not a single bird, not a single tree, is missing God. They are all enjoying life in its utter beauty and simplicity with no fear of hell and no greed for heaven, no philosophical differences. There are no Catholic lions, there are no Protestant or Hindu lions.

The whole existence must be laughing at man, at what has happened to human beings. If birds can live without religions and churches and mosques and temples, why can't man? The birds never fight religious wars; neither do the animals nor the trees. But you are a Mohammedan and I am a Hindu and we cannot coexist—either you have to become converted to my religion or be ready; I will send you to heaven immediately!

If instinct is praised, these religions lose any rationale, any reason to exist, so they praise intellect.

And the third thing, which is your future, is intuition. So these three words have to be understood.

Instinct is physical—your past, based on the experience of millions of years, infallible, never commits any mistake and does miracles in you of which you are not even aware. How does your food become blood? How does your breathing go on functioning even when you are asleep? How does your body separate the oxygen from nitrogen? How does your instinctive world of nature go on giving to every part of your body what it needs? How much oxygen is needed in your head for the mind to function? The exact amount is sent through blood running all around the body, distributing fresh oxygen, taking out the old, used, dead cells, replacing them with new ones and taking them back to places from where they can be disposed of.

The scientists say that what instinct does for man, we are not yet capable of doing. And in a small body the instinct does so many miracles. If someday science wanted to do the work of a single human body, it would need at least one square mile of factory for a single human being. Tremendous machinery! And still it will not be infallible; machinery can break, can stop, the electricity can go off. But for seventy years continuously, or even one hundred years for a few people, the instinct goes on functioning perfectly well. The electricity never goes off. Not a single mistake is committed; everything goes according to plan, and the plan is in every cell of your body. The day we can read the code of the human cells, we will be able to predict everything about a child even before he is born, even before he is in the mother's womb. The cells of the parents have a program, and in that program your age, your health, what kind of diseases you will have, your genius, your intelligence, your talents, your whole destiny is contained.

Like instinct, at the other polarity of your being—beyond the mind, which is the world of intellect—is the world of intuition.

Intuition opens its doors through meditation. Meditation is simply a knocking on the doors of intuition. Intuition is also completely ready. It does not grow; you have inherited that too from existence. Intuition is your consciousness, your being.

Intellect is your mind. Instinct is your body. And just as instinct functions perfectly on behalf of the body, intuition functions perfectly as far as your consciousness is concerned. Intellect is just between these two—a passage to be passed, a bridge to be crossed. But there are many people, many millions of people, who never cross the bridge. They simply sit on the bridge thinking they have arrived home.

The home is on the farther shore, beyond the bridge. The bridge joins instinct and intuition. But it all depends on you. You may start making a house on the bridge—then you have gone astray.

Intellect is not going to be your home. It is a small instrument, to be used only for passing from instinct to intuition. So only the person who uses his intellect to go beyond it can be called intelligent.

Intuition is existential. Instinct is natural. Intellect is just groping in the dark. The faster you move beyond intellect, the better; intellect can be a barrier to those who think nothing is beyond it. Intellect can be a beautiful passage for those who understand that there is certainly something beyond it.

> Science has stopped at intellect—that's why it cannot figure out anything about consciousness. The intellect without your intuition awake is one of the most dangerous things in the world.

Science has stopped at intellect—that's why it cannot figure out anything about consciousness. The intellect without your intuition awake is one of the most dangerous things in the world. And we are living under the dangers of intellect because intellect has given science immense power. But the power is in the hands of children, not in the hands of wise people.

Intuition makes a man wise—call it enlightenment, call it awakening; those are simply different names for wisdom. Only in the hands of wisdom can intellect be used as a beautiful servant.

And instinct and intuition function together perfectly well— one on the physical level, another on the spiritual level. The whole problem of humanity is getting stuck in the middle, in the mind, in the intellect. Then you will have misery and you will have anxiety and you will have agony and you will have meaningless-ness and you will have all kinds of tensions without any solution anywhere to be seen.

Intellect makes everything a problem and knows no solution at all. Instinct never creates any problem and does not need any solution; it simply functions naturally. Intuition is pure solution, it has no problems. Intellect is only problems, it has no solution.

If you rightly see the division, it is simple to understand: unless instinct is available, you will be dead. And unless intuition is avail-able, your life has no meaning—you just drag on. It is a kind of vegetation.

Intuition brings meaning, splendor, joy, blessings. Intuition gives you the secrets of existence, brings a tremendous silence, serenity, which cannot be disturbed and which cannot be taken away from you.

With instinct and intuition functioning together, you can also use your intellect for right purposes. Otherwise you have only means but no ends. Intellect has no idea of any ends. This has created today's situation in the world—science goes on producing things but it does not know why. Politicians go on using those things not knowing that they are destructive, that they are preparing for a global suicide. The world needs a tremendous rebellion that can take it beyond intellect into the silences of intuition.

> ✍
>
> With instinct and intuition functioning together, you can use your intellect for right purposes. Otherwise you have only means but no ends.

The very word *intuition* has to be understood. You know the word *tuition*—tuition comes from outside, somebody teaches you, the tutor. *Intuition* means something that arises within your being; it is your potential, that's why it is called *in*tuition. Wisdom is never borrowed, and that which is borrowed is never wisdom. Unless you have your own wisdom, your own vision, your own clarity, your own eyes to see, you will not be able to understand the mystery of existence.

As far as I am concerned, I am in absolute favor of instinct. Don't disturb it.

Every religion has been teaching you to disturb it—what is fasting but disturbing your instinct? Your body is hungry and asking for food, and you are starving it for spiritual reasons. A strange kind of spirituality has been possessing your being. It should be called simply stupidity, not spirituality. Your instinct is asking for water, it is thirsty; your body needs it. But your religions . . . Jainism does not allow anybody even to drink water in the night. Now as far as the body is concerned, it may feel thirsty, particularly in summer in a hot country like India—and Jainas exist only in India. In my childhood, I used to feel guilty because I had to steal water in the night. I could not sleep without drinking at least once a night in hot summers, but I used to feel that I was doing something that should not be done, that I was committing a sin. Strange and stupid ideas are being forced on people.

I am in favor of the instinct. And this is one of the secrets I want to reveal to you: if you are in total favor of instinct, it will be easy to find the way toward intuition. Because they are both the same, even though functioning on different levels—one functions on the material level, another functions on the spiritual level. To accept your instinctive life with absolute joy, without any guilt, will help you to open the doors of intuition—because they are not different, just their planes are different. And just as instinct functions beautifully, silently, without any noise, so does intuition function—and even more silently, far more beautifully.

> To accept your instinctive life with absolute joy, without any guilt, will help you to open the doors of intuition—because they are not different, just their planes are different.

Intellect is a disturbance. But it depends on us whether we make it a disturbance or use it as a stepping-stone. When you come across a stone in the street, you can either think of it as a hindrance or use it as a stepping-stone to a higher plane. Those who really understand use intellect as a stepping-stone. But the masses are under the control of religions that teach them, "Use your intellect as a repressive force for instinct." People get involved in fighting with instinct and forget all about intuition. Their whole energy becomes involved in fighting with their own life force. And when you are continuously fighting with your instinct . . .

A Jaina monk is supposed to remain naked all the year round, even in the winter months, even in the cold night. He cannot use a mattress, he cannot use a blanket, he cannot use anything to cover his body, day or night. He has to fast. The longer he fasts, the greater a saint he becomes in the eyes of the same kind of conditioned people—thirty days, forty days. . . . This is fighting against the body. This is conquering the body and the material, this is spirit conquering the body. It is the same situation in all the religions, with different superstitions. They turn the energy of your intellect against your instinct, and that spoils all possibilities of opening the flower of your intuition.

Intuition is the mystic rose that will lead you to the ultimate ecstasy and to immortal life. But people seem to be absolutely in the hands of the dead past. Whatever the old scriptures have told them, they go on doing it, without ever considering the whole science of man.

These three are the layers of the whole science of man. Instinct should be allowed a relaxed flow. Never disturb it with the intellect for any reason. And intellect should be used as an opening for intuition. It has just to give way for intuition to take over your life. Then your life is a life of immense light, of luminosity. It becomes a constant festival.

THREE RUNGS OF A LADDER

Intuition is the highest rung of the ladder, the ladder of consciousness. It can be divided into three divisions: the lowest and the first is instinct; the second, the middle one, is intellect; and the third, the highest one, is intuition.

The word *in* is used in all three words. It is significant. It means these are qualities inborn. You cannot learn them, there is no way to grow them with any outside help.

Instinct is the world of the animals—everything is instinct. Even if sometimes you see indications of other things, it is your projection. For example, you can see love in animals—the mother looking after her kids lovingly, caringly—and you can think that it is not just instinct, it is something higher, not just biological. But it is not higher, it is simply biological. The mother is doing it like a robot in the hands of nature. She is helpless—she has to do it.

In many animals the father has no instinctive fatherliness; on the contrary, many will kill their own kids and eat them. For example, in crocodiles, the life of the kids is in immense danger. The mother is protective and fights for the kids' lives, but the father just wants to have a good breakfast! The father has no instinct to be fatherly; in fact the father is a human institution. The mother crocodile has to keep the kids in her mouth to protect them from the father. She has a big mouth—all women have big mouths—she can manage to keep almost a dozen kids in her mouth. In the mother's mouth, just beside her dangerous teeth, the kids are perfectly safe. The more difficult thing is for the kids to figure out who is the mother and who is the father, because they both look alike. And sometimes the kids go close to the father, go into his mouth, and are gone forever; then they will never see the light again.

But the mother tries to fight, to protect. Perhaps that's why nature gives crocodile children in such abundance: the mother has one dozen each time, each year. If she can manage to save even two, that keeps the population exactly the same, but she manages to protect almost half of the kids.

Anybody watching will feel that the father is really cruel, has no compassion, no love, and that the mother is really motherly. But you are just projecting your ideas. The mother is protecting not for any conscious reason; it is in her hormones to protect them, and the father has nothing to do with those hormones. If he is injected with the same hormones, then he will stop killing his own kids. So it is a question of chemistry, not of psychology or of anything higher than biochemistry.

Ninety percent of man's life is still part of the animal world. We live by instinct.

You fall in love with a woman, or a woman falls in love with you, and you think it is something great. It is nothing great, it is simple instinctive infatuation: it is hormones being attracted by the opposite hormones. You are just a plaything in the hands of nature. No animal bothers about the delicacies and subtleties of love, but man feels that to be just instinctive is insulting, humiliating. Your love is just biochemistry? Your love is poetry, your love is art, your love is philosophy—but biochemistry? It seems as if you are ashamed of your biology, of your chemistry, of your nature.

But this is not the way of understanding. You have to understand exactly what is what. Distinctions have to be clear, otherwise you will remain always confused. Your ego will go on making you project as high as possible things that have nothing to do with anything higher than the lowest stratum.

> If the romantic idea of love were taken away, then I don't think any man or woman would be able to stand sex and its absurdity. It would look so stupid.

Your love is just an illusion created by your chemistry. Just think: if the romantic idea of love were taken away, then I don't think any man or woman would be able to stand sex and its absurdity. It would look so stupid. Just take away the romantic idea and think in straight terms of biology and chemistry; then your sex will make you feel ashamed. There is nothing in it to brag about. Just imagine yourself making love to a man or a woman with no romance, with no poetry, no Omar Khayyám, no Shelley, no Byron—just as a reproduction process because nature wants to procreate through you, because nature knows you are going to die. You are not permanent; before you die, nature wants life to continue. But man cannot go into sex unless he has something romantic about it, so he has created great smoke around sex, which he calls love. He pretends, even believes that it is love—but watch more carefully.

You are interested in a man or a woman. The natural instinct in a woman is to play hide-and-seek. It is strange that in all the cultures, all over the world, the small kids play two games without fail. Their religions are different, their cultures are different, their races are different, their societies, their languages—everything is different—but as far as these two games are concerned, whether they are born in Africa or China or America or India, it makes no difference. One is the game of hide-and-seek. It is strange why, all over the world, not a single culture has existed where children have not played the game of hide-and-seek. It seems to be something to do with instinct, as if they are preparing for some bigger game of hide-and-seek. This is just a rehearsal, and then for the whole of life the game is continued.

The woman is always the one who tries to hide, and the man is always the macho who seeks. It is a challenge for him to seek— the more the woman hides, the more he is challenged and excited.

But all children, all over the world, play the game of hide-and-seek. Nobody teaches them, so how did it become universal? It must be coming out from their inner nature—some urge to seek, to find, some challenge.

These things happen naturally—nobody decides these things, they are part of your biological nature. But nature has been wise enough to give you the delusion of love; otherwise, just for reproduction purposes, for life to continue, you are not going to do all those exercises and eighty-four sex postures that Vatsyayana prescribes—strange, ugly, stupid. If you take love away, then bare sex looks really animal-like. That is one of the problems that humanity has been troubled by all along, and is still troubled by. One can only hope that in the future we can make it more understandable.

The man goes on seeking, persuading, writing love letters, sending presents and doing everything in his power; but once his sex is satisfied, he starts becoming uninterested. Now, it is not something that he is doing knowingly. He does not want to hurt; particularly the person whom he has loved he does not want to hurt. But this is the way of biology. All that romance and all the love was just smoke in which nature was trying to hide the sexual part, which in itself looks ugly, so it was giving it a beautiful cover.

But once nature's work is done through you, all that smoke disappears. Instinct knows only sex. Love is only a sugarcoating on a bitter pill just to help you swallow it. Don't go on keeping it in your mouth, otherwise you will not be able to swallow it; soon the thin coating of sugar will be gone and you are going to spit out the bitter pill.

Hence lovers are in a great hurry to make love. What is the hurry? Why can't they wait? The sugar is thin and they are afraid that, if it is too late, the sugar may be gone and then it is all bitter, really bitter.

Instinct does not make you human, it simply keeps you an animal—two-legged, but still you are an animal.

The second rung, intellect, gives you something that is higher than biology, chemistry, the animal nature. Intellect is also inborn, just as intuition is, just as instinct is. There is no way to increase your intellectual capacity; all that can be done is to make your whole potential actual, which will look as if your intellect has grown. The reality is that the

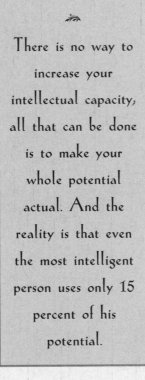

There is no way to increase your intellectual capacity; all that can be done is to make your whole potential actual. And the reality is that even the most intelligent person uses only 15 percent of his potential.

most intelligent person uses only 15 percent of his potential; the normal, ordinary, common person uses only 6 to 7 percent. Eighty-five percent of intelligence remains unused even in Albert Einstein or Bertrand Russell. That 85 percent can be made available, and it will be a tremendous growth. You will think that certainly you have grown in intelligence. But you have simply recovered, reclaimed, what was already yours.

We have found ways to teach intellect and to increase your power of memory. All the schools, colleges, and universities—the whole system of education around the world is only doing one thing: sharpening your intellect. But there has arisen a problem, which was not foreseen by the educationists. When your intellect becomes a little powerful, it starts interfering with your instinct. A competition, a struggle for power starts.

The intellect tries to dominate, and because it has logic on its side—reason, argument, a thousand and one proofs—it can manage, as far as your conscious mind is concerned, to convince you that the instinct is something evil. That's why all the religions have been condemning instinct.

They are just intellectual games—instinct is part of your unconscious mind and intellect is part of your conscious mind, but the problem is that the conscious mind is only one-tenth of the unconscious mind. It is just like an iceberg: only one-tenth shows above water, nine times more is hidden underneath. Your conscious mind is only a tenth part, but it shows; you know about it. You don't know anything about your unconscious mind.

The conscious mind is being taught in the schools, in the colleges, in the universities, in the churches, in the synagogues—everywhere. And they fill your conscious mind *against* instinct.

> ❧
>
> Whatever you decide with your conscious mind can simply be thrown away by the unconscious at any moment, because it is nine times more powerful. It does not bother about your logic.

This is an ugly phenomenon; they are making you antinature, antiyourself.

But the unconscious mind is always silent; it is deep in darkness. It is not worried about your conscious mind at all. Whatever you decide with your conscious mind can simply be thrown away by the unconscious at any moment, because it is nine times more powerful. It does not bother about your logic, your reason, or anything.

It is not without reason that even a man like Gautam Buddha was against giving women initiation into his commune. He wanted it to be purely a male commune with no female in it. I am against his attitude, but I understand what the reason was. His reason has to be thought about. He was aware that once women are there, then what are you going to do with the unconscious minds of the men? It was a question of psychology, not of religion.

Sigmund Freud or Jung or Adler are just pygmies before Gautam Buddha. It looks inhuman to prevent women, but if you look into his insight, you will be surprised; the man had some solid ground. The ground was not the woman; he was not really saying to keep the woman out. He was saying, "I know you cannot be victorious over your unconscious." In reality it was not a condemnation of women, it was a condemnation of the disciples. He was saying that in bringing the woman in, a situation is created where your unconscious will start overpowering you.

He tried every possible way to prevent that from happening. He told his monks that they had to walk looking only four feet ahead so they could not see the face of a woman on the road or anywhere; at the most they might see her legs. He told his monks, "Don't touch a woman, don't talk to a woman." One of his disciples was persistent. He said, "In some situation—for example, a woman has fallen on the road and is sick or dying—do you want us not to talk to her, to ask her where she wants to go? Do you want us not to touch her and take her to her home?"

Buddha said, "In rare situations like this, yes, you can touch her and you can talk to her—but be very aware that she is a woman."

Now his insistence "be very aware" is not against the woman, it is against your unconscious. If you are very aware, then your unconscious may not be able to penetrate and overpower the conscious mind.

All the religions have been against the woman—not that they were woman haters, no; they were simply trying to protect the monk, the priest, and the popes. Of course, I don't agree with their methodology because this is not a way to protect; in fact this makes you more inflammable. A monk who has not touched a woman, who has not talked to a woman, and who has no idea about women, is bound to be more in the grip of his instinct than a man who has lived with women, talked with them, and has been as much at ease with them as with any man.

The monks and nuns have been *more* in the power of the instinct. If you split your instinct completely from satisfaction, it

can become so powerful—almost like a drug—that it can intox-
icate you, it can make you hallucinate. And in the Middle Ages
there were monks who confessed before the special court that the
pope had convened. It was a grand jury court where all honest
nuns and monks were called and asked to confess: "Are you having
intercourse with devils, with witches?" And thousands of them
confessed, "Yes, the witches come in the night, the devils come
in the night."

The monastery walls and locks could not prevent them coming in, of course; they were devils and witches! The monks and
nuns described exactly how a witch looks, how a devil looks, and
how they were tempted into sexuality and were unable to resist.
These nuns and monks were burned alive so that it became a
lesson for others.

But nobody has bothered to look: no witch comes to you,
even if you keep your door open. No devil comes to you. Why
were these devils and witches coming only to Catholics?—strange!
What have poor Catholics done wrong?

The reason is simple. They repressed sex so much that it became a boiling-hot thing inside the unconscious. And when they
went to sleep, their dreams were so vivid and colorful and realistic—it depended on how much they had been deprived. Just fast
for two or three days and you will see: each night you will have
a beautiful feast in your dream. And as the fast goes deeper and
makes you more hungry, your feast will become more and more
delicious, fragrant, colorful, realistic. After twenty-one days of fasting you might even dream of food with open eyes, fully awake.
There is no need for sleep anymore; now the unconscious starts
infiltrating into the conscious even while you are awake. Many of

the nuns and the monks admitted that it was not only in the night; in the day also devils and witches came to visit them and made love to them. And they were unable to do anything, it was simply beyond their capacity.

Other religions have done the same thing.

My effort is just the opposite of all the religions, because I can see what they have done. The intention was good but their understanding was not deep enough. I want women and men to live together, to be acquainted with each other's bodies, differences, polarities, so that there is no need for your unconscious to carry something repressed in it.

Once your unconscious is completely free of repression, your instinct has a different quality to it. It is joined with intelligence. When your unconscious is no longer repressed, when there is no Berlin Wall between your conscious and your unconscious—the wall can be withdrawn because there is no repression, so there is no need to keep the unconscious hidden—then you can move in and out of your unconscious as easily as you move from one room to another room in your house.

This is your house—Gurdjieff used to use this metaphor of the house, that man is a three-story house. The first story is the unconscious, the second story is the conscious, the third story is the superconscious. Once your intelligence and instinct have no conflict, you become human for the first time; you are no longer part of the animal kingdom. And to me this is what is absolutely needed for anybody who wants to know truth, life, existence, for one who wants to know who he is.

In repressing nine parts of your own mind, how are you going to know yourself? You have repressed so much of yourself in a basement, where you cannot bear to go. All religious people have lived in fear, trembling. What was their fear? The fear was of their own unconscious and their repressed instincts, which were knocking on the door of their conscious: "Open the door, we want to come in! We want realization, we want to be fulfilled." The more starved they are, the more dangerous they are. You are surrounded by hungry wolves—each instinct becomes a hungry wolf. And this is the torture in which so-called religious people have lived, surrounded by hungry wolves.

I want you to be friendly with your unconscious. Let your biology be satisfied to its full. Just try to see the point: if your biology is completely satisfied, there is no fight between the conscious and the unconscious. You become one whole, as far as your mind is concerned; your mind will be one whole. It will release tremendous intelligence in you, because most of your intelligence is involved in repressing. You are sitting on a volcano, trying to keep the volcano from exploding. The volcano is going to explode—your power is so small it cannot hold it forever; on the contrary, when it explodes, you will be thrown into such small pieces that to put you together again will be impossible.

The many mad people around the world, in your mad asylums, hospitals—what are they? Who are they? What has gone wrong with

> *Most of your intelligence is involved in repressing. You are sitting on a volcano, trying to keep the volcano from exploding.*

them? They have fallen in pieces and you can't put them together. There is no possibility of putting them together unless you arrange for all their repressed instincts to be fulfilled. But who is there even to say this? Because I have been saying it for all of thirty-five years, I have become the most notorious man in the world.

Just the other day in the German *Stern* magazine, I saw a cover story of fifteen pages about my commune, and this is only the first part of a series. It is going to be in five parts, in five consecutive issues of the magazine. Their heading on the title page is "The Sex State." I really liked it! And the strangest thing is, if you go on looking beyond those fifteen pages, then you will be surprised. Who is living in a sex state? The *Stern* staff, their editors, and their board members, or us?

In the magazine are nude women—and they are not just naked, because a totally naked woman is not so fascinating. You have to make her nakedness even more fascinating by giving her sexual clothes, which in a way show her body and in a way hide it too. So you can play the hide-and-seek game again. You can start dreaming about how the woman looks behind these clothes. She may not be so beautiful behind these clothes—in fact all female bodies are the same and all male bodies are the same, once you put the light off and all colorfulness and all differences disappear. Darkness is such an equalizer, so communistic, that in darkness you can even love your own wife.

The whole magazine is full of sex, but *we* are "the sex state." Even *Playboy* writes against me—I wonder what a really strange world we are living in! But I know why *Stern* or *Playboy* or magazines like that, which are third-rate and exploiting people's sexuality . . . they are sold in millions. *Stern* sells almost 2 million copies, and each copy is estimated to be read by at least eight people; that means 16 million readers.

Why should they be against me? And they have been against me for years. The reason is that if I succeed, then these magazines will have to close their offices. They live upon repression. It is a simple logic, why they are against me. The priests, who are against sex, are against me, and the people who are using sex as an exploitation—*Playboy, Stern,* and there are thousands of magazines around the world—they are also against me. It seems strange, because they are not against the pope; there is not a single article against the pope. *Playboy* should be against the pope, who is continually condemning sex. But no . . .

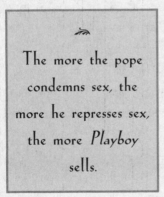

The more the pope condemns sex, the more he represses sex, the more *Playboy* sells.

There is an intrinsic logic: the more the pope condemns sex, the more he represses sex, the more *Playboy* sells. Only in my commune will nobody be interested in *Playboy* or *Stern*—who bothers? If I succeed, then all these pornographic magazines, literature, and movies are simply bound to disappear. And there is a great investment behind them, so they will all oppose me—and they will oppose me and condemn me in the name of sex, as if I am spreading sexuality.

If anybody has spread sexuality, it must be your God. I have nothing to do with it. He goes on giving birth to children with sex hormones. He should stop it—he should listen to the pope! But these magazines are not against God either, because he is providing the whole market. Popes and pornographers are all in a deep conspiracy—and they are together against me because I am simply trying to spoil the game.

Both these types of people are exploiting repression; hence, it is logical in every way to be against me—they are both against me. At least *Stern* should not be against me if I have created a sex state; they should be happy and they should be favorable. But no, they are absolutely angry. They may not even be aware why they are angry with me; they may be doing it absolutely unconsciously, but the unconscious also has its own reasons.

Repress anything and it becomes valuable. Repress more, and it becomes more valuable. Don't repress and it loses all value.

Express it, it evaporates.

I can say to the world that my commune is the only place where sex means nothing; it has no value. Nobody is bothered by it; nobody is dreaming about it and nobody is fantasizing about it. In fact, people continually write to me, "Osho, what to do? My sex life is completely disappearing."

I say, "What to do? Let it disappear. You need not do anything. This is the whole purpose here: it *should* disappear! Don't make any effort to make it disappear, but when it is disappearing, please, don't make any effort to prevent it. Say good-bye. It is just great that it is disappearing." But the trouble is that people think that when sex is disappearing, perhaps now nothing is left because sex was all their excitement, their ecstasy, and their joy.

No, there is really so much waiting for you. Just let sex disappear so that your energy becomes available for a higher kind of excitement, a higher kind of ecstasy.

When your unconscious and conscious meet because there is

nothing repressed in the unconscious—and that is the moment of their meeting and their merger—at that very moment another great opportunity opens up for you. Because you are no longer involved with the lower, your whole energy is available for the higher.

You are in the middle, the conscious mind. But because the unconscious is there, you remain involved in repressing it, you go on repressing it—it is not a question that once you have repressed it, you are finished with it. You have to repress it constantly, because it is coming up again and again.

> Energy has a fundamental principle about it: it cannot remain static, it has to move. Movement is its nature.

It is just like bouncing a ball. You throw it and it comes back to you. The greater force you put into hitting it, the greater is the force with which it comes toward you. The same is the situation with instincts. You repress them, and the more energy you put in repressing, the more energy they will have coming back to you. From where can they get energy? It is your energy. But when you are completely free from the unconscious and its involvements, it is clean and silent; then your whole energy is available.

Energy has a fundamental principle about it: it cannot remain static, it has to move. Movement is its nature. It is not a thing that you put somewhere and it remains there. No, it has to move—it is life. So when there is no reason to move downward, it has only one way to move—upward. There is nowhere else to go. It starts hitting your superconscious, and just its hit to the superconscious is so pleasant and such a joy that all your sexual orgasms simply pale. You cannot imagine it, because it is not a quantitative difference such that I can tell you that "it is ten thousand times greater in quantity." The difference is of *quality,* so there is no way to imagine it. How to compare it to your sexual orgasm? But that is the only thing in your life through which something higher can be indicated.

When your energy starts hitting your upper world, of which you were not even aware up to now, there is a constant showering of joy. The sexual orgasm is so momentary that by the time you know it is there, it is gone. You only remember it in memory; you don't really realize when it is there. Because of this momentariness you become more and more addicted to it, because you remember there was something, something great was happening, so, "Let us go into it again, let us go into it again." But there is no way. . . .

Before it comes—you know it is coming because the bell starts ringing in your head. It is really a bell that starts ringing in your head: "It is coming!" You know that it is coming . . . you know that it is gone. The bell has stopped, it is not ringing anymore, and you look like a fool! Between the ringing of the bell and the stopping of the bell, you look like a fool. Perhaps the man feels more ashamed; that's why after making love he simply turns and goes to sleep. The woman is not that much ashamed for the simple reason that she is not such an active partner; the man looks foolish because he is the active partner.

Just the energy touching your higher level of consciousness, the superconscious—just the touch, and there is a shower of joy, which continues. Slowly the energy goes on hitting and makes its way to the center of the superconsciousness. You have nothing to do: your work is finished when you have stopped repressing and you have cleaned your unconscious. Then you have nothing to do; then all that has to be done is done by your energy. And when you reach the center, a new faculty starts functioning in you, which is intuition.

At the center of the unconscious is instinct.

At the center of the conscious is intellect.

At the center of the superconscious is intuition.

Instinct makes you do things, forces you to do things even against your will. Intellect helps you to find ways if you want to do a certain thing, or to find ways if you don't want to do a certain thing. Intellect's function is to find a way.

If you want to go *with* the instinct, intellect will find a way. If you are a so-called religious person, a pseudoreligious person, and you want to go *against* your instinct, intellect will find a way. They may be strange ways, but intellect is at your service: whatever you want, it will do. It is not in favor of or against anything, it is simply at your disposal.

If a man is sane, he will use his intellect to help his unconscious be fulfilled. The sooner it is fulfilled the better, so that you are free from it. Fulfillment means freedom from it.

If you are some kind of crackpot—Catholic, Protestant, any kind, there are all sorts of crackpots available in the world. You can choose what kind of crackpot you want to be, Hindu, Mohammedan, Jaina, Buddhist—all kinds of varieties are available. You cannot say, "The variety I want is not available"—you cannot say that; in thousands of years, man has created almost every single variety of crackpot. You can choose, you can have your choice; but whatever you choose, it is the same.

Nobody has told you how to use intellect to fulfill your unconscious, your nature, your biology, your chemistry. They are yours—what does it matter whether it is chemistry or biology or physiology? They are part of you, and nature never gives anything without reason. Fulfill it, and its fulfillment is going to make a path for the higher potential.

All religious people are hung up with the lowest part of their being— that's why they look so sad and so guilty. They cannot rejoice. Jesus goes on saying to these people, "Rejoice," and on the other hand he goes on saying to them, "Remember hell." He is creating a dilemma for people! Showing them the way to hell—the way to hell is to fulfill your nature and the way to heaven is to go against your nature.

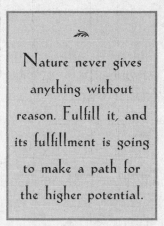

Nature never gives anything without reason. Fulfill it, and its fulfillment is going to make a path for the higher potential.

But to go against your nature creates hell here on earth.

I want to create paradise here, now. Why postpone such a good thing?

Things that are not worth your attention you can postpone— but paradise? I am not ready to postpone it for tomorrow or for the next second. You can have it here, now; all that you need is a clean unconscious. Fulfilled, contented, biology settles, chemistry settles, and gives you all the energy that was involved in those planes. The energy shoots upward by itself, and it stops only at the very center of your superconscious mind. And there intuition starts functioning.

What is intuition? Intuition is in some ways like instinct, in some ways absolutely unlike instinct; in some ways like intellect, in other ways absolutely against intellect. So you will have to understand, because it is the subtlest thing in you.

Intuition is like instinct because you cannot do anything about it. It is part of your consciousness, just as instinct is part of your body. You cannot do anything about your instinct and you cannot do anything about your intuition. But just as you can allow your instincts to be fulfilled, you can allow and give total freedom to your intuition to be fulfilled. And you will be surprised at what kinds of powers you have been carrying within you.

Intuition can give you answers for ultimate questions—not verbally but existentially.

You need not ask, "What is truth?"—instinct won't hear, it is deaf. Intellect will hear, but it can only philosophize; it is blind, it can't see. Intuition is a *seer,* it has eyes. It *sees* the truth, there is no question of thinking about it.

Instinct and intuition are both independent of you. Instinct is in the power of nature, of unconscious nature, and intuition is in the hands of the superconscious universe. That consciousness surrounds the whole universe, is the oceanic consciousness of which we are just small islands—or better, icebergs, because we can melt into it and become one with it.

In some ways intuition is exactly opposite to instinct. Instinct always leads you to the other; its fulfillment is always dependent on something other than you. Intuition leads you only to yourself. It has no dependence, no need for the other; hence its beauty, its freedom and independence. Intuition is an exalted state needing nothing. It is so full of itself that there is no space for anything else.

In some way intuition is like intellect because it is intelligence. Intellect and intelligence are similar at least in appearance, but only in appearance. The intellectual person is not necessarily intelligent, and the intelligent person is not necessarily intellectual. You can find a farmer so intelligent that even a great professor, a great intellectual, will look like a pygmy in front of him.

It happened in Soviet Russia after the Revolution that they changed the city of Petrograd to make it a new city named after Lenin, Leningrad. In front of Petrograd's huge, beautiful, and ancient castle there was a big rock, which the czars had never thought to remove—there was no need. Now cars had come into existence, and that rock was blocking the road, it had to be removed.

But the rock was so beautiful that they wanted to remove it and keep it as a memorial, so they did not want to destroy it or dynamite it. But all the great engineers—all they could think about was to dynamite it or to start cutting it up piece by piece and then later on to put the pieces together. But Lenin said, "That won't do—that will not be the same thing. The rock is so beautiful, that's why the czars have kept it just in front of their palace."

At that point a man came, a poor man on his donkey. He stood there listening to all this argument; then he laughed and started moving on. Lenin said, "Wait, why did you laugh?"

The man said, "It is such a simple matter. Nothing much has to be done: all that you have to do is to dig around the rock. Don't touch the rock at all; just dig around the rock and the rock will settle deeper into the hole. You will not be disturbing the rock—the rock will remain there—but it will not be blocking anybody. There is no need to dynamite it or to destroy it."

Lenin said to his engineers, "You are great engineers and architects, but what this poor fellow is saying is more intelligent." And that's what was done. The rock was saved and the road was saved, but the idea came from a poor man who was nobody.

I have watched it, meeting thousands of people, that mostly intellectual people are not intelligent because they don't have to be intelligent. Their intellect, their knowledge, is enough. But a man who has no knowledge, no intellect and no education, has to find some intelligence within himself; he cannot look outside. And because he has to depend on intelligence, intelligence starts growing.

So intuition has something similar to intellect, but it is not intellectual. It is intelligence.

The functioning of intellect and intelligence are totally different. Intellect functions through steps, step-by-step. It has a procedure, a methodology. If you are doing a question in mathematics, then there are steps to be followed.

In India there is a woman, Shakuntala, who has been around the world in almost all the universities, exhibiting her intuition. She is not a mathematician, she is not even much educated—just a high school graduate. Even when Albert Einstein was alive, she was giving her demonstration in front of him. And her demonstration was strange. She would sit with a chalk in her hand in front of a blackboard; you would ask any kind of question about mathematics or arithmetic, and you would not even have finished the question and she would have started writing the answer.

Albert Einstein gave her a certificate—she showed the certificate to me when I was in Madras where she lives. She showed me all her certificates, and the one from Albert Einstein says, "I asked this woman a question that I take three hours to solve because I have to follow a whole method; I cannot just jump from the question to the answer. I know that nobody can do it in less time than I can, and that is three hours. Others may take even six hours or more, but I can do it in three hours because I have done it before. But the whole procedure has to be followed. If you miss even a single step . . ." The figures were so big that it took the whole board for her to write the answer. And before Einstein had even finished the question, she had started writing the answer.

He was puzzled, absolutely puzzled, because it was impossible. He asked, "How do you do it?"

She said, "I don't know how I do it—it simply happens. You ask me and figures start appearing before my eyes, somewhere inside. I can see 1, 2, 3, and I just go on writing."

That woman was born with her intuition functioning. But I felt really sad for her because she became just an exhibition. Nobody cared that a woman who is born with intuition functioning can become enlightened easily. She is just standing on the border; one step and she becomes the ultimate in consciousness. But she is not aware, because this is just some freak of nature.

There was another boy, Shankaran, who used to pull a ricksha in the city. A professor of mathematics, an Englishman, used to go in Shankaran's ricksha to the university. Once or twice it happened that the professor was thinking about some problem, and the boy simply looked at him and said, "This is the answer." The professor

> Intuition functions in a quantum leap. It has no methodological procedure, it simply sees things. It has eyes to see.

had not spoken—he was simply thinking—and the boy was pulling the ricksha, but he said, "This is the answer."

The professor went to the university, worked out the whole process, and was surprised that this was the answer. When it happened two or three times, he asked the boy, "How do you do it?"

He said, "I don't do anything. I just feel you behind me, worried, and some figures start appearing. I am not much educated, but figures I can understand. And I see so many figures in your mind, just behind me—a line, a queue— and then suddenly a few figures appear in my mind, so I tell you that this is the answer. I don't know how it happens."

The professor sent Shankaran to Oxford, because he was even more advanced than this woman Shakuntala. You had to ask her the question, then she could write; with Shankaran you just had to visualize the question in your mind and he would write the answer. His intuition was functioning more fully, he was seeing both the answer and the question—he could read your mind. And he was even more illiterate, so poor a man that he was pulling a ricksha. He became a phenomenon in the history of mathematics because many questions that had remained unsolved for centuries, he solved—although he could not say how. He gave the answer— but how to judge whether the answer was right or wrong? It took many years. When a higher mathematics was developed, then they could work it out. Shankaran was dead, but his answers were right.

Intuition functions in a quantum leap.

It has no methodological procedure, it simply sees things.

It has eyes to see.

It sees things that you have never even thought of as things— for example, love. You have never thought of it as a thing. But a man of intuition can see whether there is love in you or not, whether there is trust in you or not, whether there is doubt in you or not. He can see them as if these are things.

In my vision, intuition holds the highest place. That's where I am trying to push you.

> An unclean unconscious is hindering you. Clean it, and the way to clean it is to satisfy it, to satisfy it so much that it starts telling you, "Please stop! It is more than I needed." Only leave it then.

An unclean unconscious is hindering you. Clean it; and the way to clean it is to satisfy it, to satisfy it so much that it starts telling you, "Please stop! It is more than I needed." Only leave it then. And with that, your intellect is filled with such a fresh flow of energy that it turns into intelligence. Then the energy goes on rising and opens the doors of intuition. Then you can see things that are not visible to your physical eyes, things that are not even things.

Love is not a thing, truth is not a thing, trust is not a thing, but they are realities—much more real than your things. But they are realities only for intuition, they are existential. And once your intuition starts functioning, you are for the first time really human.

With the unconscious you are animal. With the conscious you are no longer animal. With the superconscious you are human.

I love to quote a Baul mystic, Chandidas, because that man, in a simple statement, has condensed my whole approach: *Sabar upar manus satya; tahar upar nahin.* "Above all is the truth of man, and above that there is nothing."

This man, Chandidas, must have been an authentically religious man. He is denying God, he is denying anything above human flowering. *Sabar upar*—"above all, above everything." *Manus satya*—"the truth of man." *Tahar upar nahin*—"and beyond that I have traveled long—there is nothing."

Once you have reached to your human potential in its total flowering, you have arrived home.

BARRIERS TO KNOWING

To know means to be silent, utterly silent,
so you can hear the still, small voice within.
To know means to drop the mind.
When you are absolutely still,
unmoving, nothing wavers in you,
the doors open.
You are part of this mysterious existence.
You know it by becoming part of it,
by becoming a participant in it.
That is knowing.

KNOWLEDGE

What is the difference between knowledge and knowing? There is no difference in the dictionary, but in existence there is a tremendous difference. Knowledge is a theory, knowing is an experience. Knowing means you open your eyes and you see; knowledge means somebody else has opened his eyes and he has seen and he talks about it, and you simply go on gathering that information. Knowledge is possible even if you are blind. Knowledge is possible. . . . Without eyes you can learn many things about light, but knowing is not possible if you are blind. Knowing is possible only if your eyes are healed, cured, if you can see. Knowing is authentically your experience; knowledge is pseudo. Knowledge is a curse, a calamity, a cancer.

It is through knowledge that man becomes divided from the whole—knowledge creates the distance. You come across a wild-flower in the mountains and you don't know what it is; your mind has nothing to say about it, the mind is silent. You look at the flower, you see the flower, but no knowledge arises in you—there is wonder, there is mystery. The flower is there, you are there. Through wonder you are not separate, you are bridged. But if you know that this is a rose or a marigold or something else, that very knowledge disconnects you. The flower is there, you are here, but there is no bridge—you "know." Knowledge creates distance.

The more you know, the bigger the distance; the less you know, the lesser the distance. And if you are in a moment of not knowing, there is no distance; you are bridged.

You fall in love with a woman or a man—the day you fall in love there is no distance. There is only wonder, a thrill, an excitement, an ecstasy—but no knowledge. You don't know who this woman is. Without knowledge there is nothing to divide you; hence the beauty of those first moments of love. Once you have lived with the woman—only for twenty-four hours—knowledge has arisen. Now you have some ideas about the woman; you know who she is, there is an image. Twenty-four hours have created a past; those twenty-four hours have left marks on the mind. You look at the same woman, there is no longer the same mystery. You are coming down the hill, that peak is lost.

To understand this is to understand much. To understand that knowledge divides, knowledge creates distance, is to understand the very secret of meditation.

Meditation is a state of not knowing. Meditation is pure space, undisturbed by knowledge. Yes, the biblical story is true—that man has fallen through knowledge, by eating the fruit of the tree of knowledge. No other scripture of the world surpasses that. That parable is the last word; no other parable has reached to that height and that insight. It looks so illogical that man has fallen through knowledge. It looks illogical because logic is part of knowledge! Logic is all in support of knowledge—it looks illogical because logic is the root cause of man's fall.

A man who is absolutely logical—absolutely sane, always sane, never allows any illogic in his life—is a madman. Sanity needs to be balanced by insanity; logic needs to be balanced by illogic. The opposites meet and balance. A man who is just rational is unreasonable—he will miss much. In fact he will go on missing all that is beautiful and all that is true. He will collect trivia, his life will be a mundane life. He will be a worldly man.

That biblical parable has immense insight. Why has man fallen through knowledge? Because knowl-

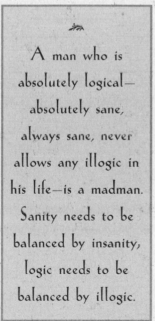

A man who is absolutely logical—absolutely sane, always sane, never allows any illogic in his life—is a madman. Sanity needs to be balanced by insanity, logic needs to be balanced by illogic.

> ⤳
>
> The child has the quality of nonknowledge, innocence. He looks with wonder, his eyes are absolutely clear. He looks deep but he has no prejudices, no judgments, no a priori ideas.

edge creates distance, because knowledge creates "I and thou," because knowledge creates subject and object, the knower and the known, the observer and the observed. Knowledge is basically schizophrenic; it creates a split and then there is no way to bridge it.

That's why the more man has become knowledgeable the less he is religious. The more educated a man, the less is the possibility for him to approach the whole. Jesus is right when he says, "Only children will be able to enter into my kingdom."

Only children . . . what is the quality that a child has and you have lost? The child has the quality of nonknowledge, innocence. He looks with wonder, his eyes are absolutely clear. He looks deep but he has no prejudices, no judgments, no a priori ideas. He does not project; hence he comes to know that which is. The child knows the truth, you know only the mundane reality. The reality is that which you have created around yourself by projecting, desiring, thinking. The reality is your interpretation of truth.

Truth is simply that which is; reality is that which you have come to understand—it is your idea of the truth. Reality consists of things, all separate. Truth consists of only one cosmic energy. Truth consists of oneness, reality consists of manyness. Reality is a crowd, truth is integration.

J. Krishnamurti has said, "To negate is silence." To negate what? To negate knowledge, to negate mind, to negate this constant occupation inside you . . . to create an unoccupied space. When you are unoccupied, you are in tune with the whole. When you are occupied, you have fallen out of tune. Hence, whenever it happens that you can attain a moment of silence, there is immense joy. In that moment life has significance, in that moment life has a grandeur beyond words. In that moment life is a dance. In that moment if even death comes, it will be a dance and a celebration because that moment knows nothing but joy. That moment is joyous, it is blissful.

Knowledge has to be negated—but not because I am saying so, or because J. Krishnamurti says so, or because Gautam Buddha has said so. If you negate because I am saying so, then you will negate your knowledge and whatsoever I am saying will become your knowledge in its place; you will substitute it. Then whatsoever I say becomes your knowledge and you start clinging to it. You throw out your old idols and you replace them with new ones, but it is the same game played with new words, new ideas, new thoughts.

Then how to negate knowledge? Not with other knowledge. Just seeing that knowledge creates distance—just seeing into this fact intensely, totally—is enough. Not that you have to replace it with something else.

That intensity is fire, that intensity will reduce your knowledge to ashes. That intensity is enough. That intensity is what is known as insight. Insight will burn your knowledge and it will not be replaced by other knowledge. Then there is emptiness, *shunyata*. Then there is nothingness, because then there is no content: there is undisturbed, undistorted truth.

You have to see what I am saying; you are not to learn what I am saying. Here, listening to me, don't start collecting knowledge. Here, don't start hoarding. Listening to me should be an experiment in insight. You should listen with intensity, with totality, with as much awareness as is possible for you. In that very awareness you will see a point, and that very seeing is transformation. Not that you have to do something else afterward; the seeing itself brings mutation.

If some effort is needed, that simply shows you missed. If you come tomorrow and ask me, "I have understood that knowledge is a curse, that knowledge creates distance. Now, how to drop it?"—then you missed. If the question how arises, then you missed. The how cannot arise, because the how is asking for more knowledge. The how is asking for methods, techniques, what should be done.

Insight is enough; it need not be helped by any efforts. Its fire is more than enough to burn all knowledge that you carry within you. Just see the point.

Listening to me, go with me. Listening to me, hold my hand and move in the spaces that I'm trying to help you to move in, and see what I am saying. Don't argue—don't say yes, don't say no; don't agree, don't disagree. Just be with me in this moment—and suddenly the insight is there. If you are listening attentively . . . and by attention I don't mean concentration; by attention I simply mean you are listening with awareness, not with a dull mind; you are listening with intelligence, with aliveness, with openness. You are here, now, with me—that's what I mean by attention. You are nowhere else. You are not comparing in your mind what I am saying with your old thoughts. You are not comparing at all, you are not judging. You are not there judging inside, within you, whether what I am saying is right or not, or how much is right.

Just the other day I was talking with a seeker. He has the quality of a seeker, but is burdened by knowledge. While I was talking to him, his eyes became full of tears. His heart was just going to open, and in that very moment the mind jumped in and destroyed the whole beauty of it. He was just moving toward the heart and opening, but immediately his mind came in. Those tears that were just on the verge of dropping disappeared. His eyes became dry. What had happened? I had said something with which he could not agree.

He was agreeing with me, up to a certain point. Then I said something that goes against his Jewish background, which goes against the Cabala, and immediately the whole energy changed. He said, "Everything is right. Whatsoever you are saying is right, but this one thing—that God has no purpose, that existence exists purposelessly—with this I cannot agree. Because the Cabala says just the opposite: that life has purpose, that God is purposive, that he is leading us toward a certain destiny, that there is a destination."

He may not even have looked at it this way—that he missed in that moment because comparison came in. What does the Cabala have to do with me? When you are with me, put away all your knowledge of the Cabala, of Yoga, of Tantra, of this and that. When you are with me, be with me. And I am not saying that you are agreeing with me, remember—there is no question of agreement or disagreement.

> When you see a rose, do you agree with it or disagree with it? When you see the sunrise, do you agree or do you disagree?

When you see a rose, do you agree with it or disagree with it? When you see the sunrise, do you agree or do you disagree? When you see the moon in the night, you simply see it! Either you see it or you don't see it, but there is no question of agreement or disagreement.

I'm not trying to convince you about anything. I'm not trying to convert you to some theory, philosophy, dogma, to some church, no. I'm simply sharing what has happened to me, and in that very sharing, if you participate, it can happen to you too. It is infectious.

Insight transforms.

When I am saying knowledge is a curse, you can agree or disagree—and you have missed! You just listen to it, just see into it, go into the whole process of knowledge. You can see how knowledge creates distance, how knowledge becomes a barrier. How knowledge stands in between, how knowledge goes on increasing and the distance goes on increasing. How innocence is lost through knowledge, how wonder is destroyed, crippled, murdered through knowledge, how life becomes a dull and boring affair through knowledge. Mystery is lost. Mystery disappears because you start having the idea that you know. When you know, how can there be mystery? Mystery is possible only when you don't know.

And remember, man has not known a thing! All that we have gathered is just rubbish. The ultimate remains beyond our grasp. What we have gathered are only facts, truth remains untouched by our efforts. And that is the experience not only of Buddha, Krishna, Krishnamurti, and Ramana; that is the experience even of Edison, Newton, Albert Einstein. That is the experience of poets, painters, dancers. All the great intelligences of the world—they may be mystics, they may be poets, they may be scientists—are in absolute agreement about one thing: that the more we know, the more we understand that life is an absolute mystery. Our knowledge does not destroy its mystery.

It is only stupid people who think that because they know a little bit, now there is no more mystery in life. It is only the mediocre mind that becomes too attached to knowledge; the intelligent mind remains above knowledge. He uses it, certainly uses it—it is useful, it is utilitarian—but knows perfectly well that all that is true is hidden, remains hidden. We can go on knowing and knowing, but the mystery remains inexhaustible.

Listen with insight, attention, totality. And in that very vision you will see something. And that seeing changes you—you don't ask how. That is the meaning when Krishnamurti says, "To negate is silence." Insight negates. And when something is negated and nothing is posited instead, something has been destroyed and nothing has been put in its place. There is silence, because there is space. There is silence because the old has been thrown out and the new has not been brought in. That silence Buddha calls *shunyata*. That silence is emptiness, nothingness. And only that nothingness can operate in the world of truth.

Thought cannot operate there. Thought works only in the world of things, because thought is also a thing—subtle, but it is also material. That's why thought can be recorded, that's why thought can be relayed, conveyed. I can throw a thought at you; you can hold it, you can have it. It can be taken and given, it is transferable because it is a thing. It is a material phenomenon.

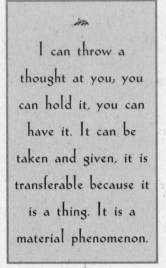

I can throw a thought at you; you can hold it, you can have it. It can be taken and given, it is transferable because it is a thing. It is a material phenomenon.

Emptiness cannot be given, emptiness cannot be thrown at you. You can participate in it, you can move into it, but nobody can give it to you. It is nontransferable. And only emptiness operates in the world of truth.

Truth is known only when mind is not. To know truth, mind has to cease; it has to stop functioning. It has to be quiet, still, unmoving.

Thought cannot operate in truth, but truth can operate through thoughts. You cannot attain to truth by thinking, but when you have attained it, you can use thinking in its service. That's what I am doing, that's what Buddha has done, that's what all the masters have done. What I am saying is a thought, but behind this thought is emptiness. That emptiness has not been produced by thought, that emptiness is beyond thought. Thought cannot touch it, thought cannot even look at it.

Have you observed one phenomenon?—that you cannot think about emptiness, you cannot make emptiness a thought. You cannot think about it, it is unthinkable. If you can think about it, it will not be emptiness at all. Thought has to go for emptiness to come; they never meet. Once emptiness has come, it can use all kinds of devices to express itself.

Insight is a state of no-thought. Whenever you see something, you always see when there is no thought. Here also, listening to me, being with me, sometimes you *see*—but those moments are gaps, intervals. One thought has gone, another has not come, and there is a gap; and in that gap something strikes, something starts vibrating. It is like somebody playing on a drum—the drum is empty inside; that's why it can be played upon. That emptiness vibrates. That beautiful sound that comes is produced out of emptiness. When you *are,* without a thought, then something is possible, immediately possible. Then you can see what I am saying. Then it will not be just a word heard, then it will become an intuition, an insight, a vision. You have looked into it, you have shared it with me.

> Insight is a state of no-thought. Whenever you see something, you always see when there is no thought.

Insight is a state of nonthinking, no-thought. It is a gap, an interval in the process of thought, and in that gap is the glimpse, the truth.

The English word *empty* comes from a root that means "at leisure," unoccupied. It is a beautiful word if you go to the root. The root is very pregnant: it means at leisure, unoccupied. Whenever you are unoccupied, at leisure, you are empty. And remember, the proverb that says that the empty mind is the devil's workshop is just nonsense. Just the opposite is the truth: the occupied mind is the devil's workshop! The empty mind is God's workshop, not the devil's. But you have to understand what I mean by "empty"—at leisure, relaxed, nontense, not moving, not desiring, not going anywhere, just being here, utterly here. An empty mind is a pure presence. And all is possible in that pure presence, because the whole existence comes out of that pure presence.

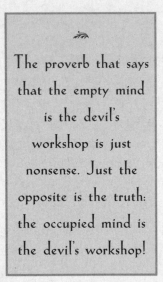

The proverb that says that the empty mind is the devil's workshop is just nonsense. Just the opposite is the truth: the occupied mind is the devil's workshop!

These trees grow out of that pure presence, these stars are born out of this pure presence; we are here—all the buddhas have come out of this pure presence. In that pure presence you are in God, you *are* God. Occupied, you fall; occupied, you have to be expelled from the Garden of Eden. Unoccupied, you are back in the Garden; unoccupied, you are back at home.

When the mind is not occupied by reality—by things, by thoughts— then there is that which is. And that which is, is the truth. Only in emptiness is there a meeting, merging. Only in emptiness do you open to truth and truth enters in you. Only in emptiness do you become pregnant with truth.

These are the three states of the mind. The first is content and consciousness. You always have contents in the mind—a thought moving, a desire arising, anger, greed, ambition. You always have some content in the mind; the mind is never unoccupied. The traffic goes on, day in, day out. While you are awake, it is there; while you sleep, it is there. Content while awake you call thinking; content while asleep you call dreaming—it is the same process. Dreaming is a little more primitive, that's all—because it thinks in pictures. It does not use concepts, it uses pictures. It is more primitive—the way small children think in pictures. So in books for small children you have to make big pictures, colorful, because they think through pictures. Through pictures they will learn words. By and by those pictures become smaller and smaller, and then they disappear.

The primitive man also thinks in pictures. The most ancient languages are pictorial languages. Chinese is a pictorial language: it has no alphabet. It is the most ancient language. In the night you again become primitive, you forget your sophistication of the day and you start thinking in pictures—but it is the same.

And the psychoanalyst's insight is valuable—that he looks into your dreams. Then there is more truth, because you are more primitive; you are not trying to deceive anybody, you are more authentic. In the day you have a personality around you that hides you—layers upon layers of personality. It is difficult to find the true man. You will have to dig deep, and it hurts, and the man will resist. But in the night, just as you put your clothes away, you put your personality away too. It is not needed because you will not be communicating with anybody, you will be alone in your bed. And you will not be in the world, you will be absolutely in your private realm. There is no need to hide and no need to pretend. That's why the psychoanalyst tries to go into your dreams, because they show much more clearly who you are. But it is the same game played in different languages; the game is not different.

This is the ordinary state of the mind: mind and content, consciousness plus content.

The second state of the mind is consciousness without content; that's what meditation is. You are fully alert, and there is a gap, an interval. No thought is encountered, there is no thought before you. You are not asleep, you are awake—but there is no thought. This is meditation. The first state is called mind, the second state is called meditation.

And then there is a third state. When the content has disappeared, the object has disappeared, the subject cannot remain for long—because they exist together. They produced each other. When the subject is alone, it can only hang around a little while more, just out of the momentum of the past. Without the content the consciousness cannot be there long; it will not be needed, because a consciousness is always a consciousness *about* something. When you say "conscious," it can be asked, "Of what?" You say, "I am conscious of . . ." That object is needed, it is a must for the subject to exist. Once the object has disappeared, soon the subject will also disappear. First go the contents, then consciousness disappears.

Then the third state is called *samadhi*—no content, no consciousness. But remember, this no-content, no-consciousness, is not a state of unconsciousness. It is a state of superconsciousness, of transcendental consciousness. Consciousness now is only conscious of itself. Consciousness has turned upon itself; the circle is complete. You have come home. This is the third state, *samadhi;* and this third state is what Buddha means by *shunyata*.

First drop the content—you become half empty. Then drop

consciousness—you become fully empty. And this full emptiness is the most beautiful thing that can happen, the greatest benediction.

INTELLECT

I am not absolutely against intellect. It has its uses—but they are limited, and you have to understand their limitations. If you are working as a scientist, you will have to use your intellect. It is a beautiful mechanism, but it is beautiful only if it remains a slave and does not become the master. If it becomes the master and overpowers you, then it is dangerous. Mind as a slave to consciousness is a beautiful servant; mind as a master of consciousness is a dangerous master.

The whole question is of emphasis. I am not absolutely against intellect—I use intellect myself, how can I be against it? Right now, talking to you, I am using it. But I am the master; it is not my master. If I want to use it, I use it. If I don't want to use it, it has no power over me. But your intellect, your mind, your thinking process, continues whether you want it to or not. It does not bother about you—as if you are nobody at all—it goes on and on; even when you are asleep,

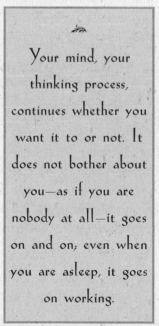

Your mind, your thinking process, continues whether you want it to or not. It does not bother about you—as if you are nobody at all—it goes on and on; even when you are asleep, it goes on working.

> You dream only because so much work has been left undone in the day that the mind has to do it. It is overtime work, you have not been able to finish in the day.

it goes on working. It does not listen to you at all. It has remained in power for so long that it has forgotten completely that it is only a servant.

When you go for a walk, you use your legs. But when you are sitting, there is no need to go on moving your legs. People ask me, "Osho, for two hours straight you go on speaking to us from your chair, in the same posture. You don't even move your legs once." Why should I move? I am not walking! But I know you—even if you are sitting on your chair, you are not really sitting. You are moving your legs, changing your positions, postures, doing a thousand and one things, tossing and turning, a great restlessness. The same is true about your mind.

If I am talking to you, I am using the mind. The moment I stop talking, my mind stops too, immediately! If I am not talking to you, my mind has no need to go on working, it simply goes into silence. That's how it should be—it should be natural. While asleep, I don't dream; there is no need. You dream only because so much work has been left undone in the day that the mind has to do it. It is overtime work; you have not been able to finish in the day.

And how can you finish anything? You are doing a thousand and one things simultaneously. Nothing is ever finished; everything remains incomplete—and remains incomplete forever. You will die, but nothing will be complete. Not even in a single direction will your work be complete because you are running in all the directions. You have become many fragments, you are not integrated. The mind is dragging you into one thing, the heart is dragging you into another, the body wants you to go somewhere else, and you are always at a loss—to whom to listen? And the mind is also not one, you have many minds—you are multi-psychic, there is a crowd of minds in you. There is no unity, no harmony. You are not an orchestra—nothing is in tune. Everything is going on its own; nobody listens to anybody else—you simply create noise, not music.

Intellect is good if it functions as a servant of the whole. Nothing is bad if it is in its right place, and everything is wrong if it is in the wrong place. Your head is perfectly good if it is on your shoulders. If it is somewhere else, then it is wrong.

Working as a scientist, intellect is needed. Working in the marketplace, the intellect is needed. Communicating with words, talking to people, the intellect is needed. But it has a limited use. There are far greater things where intellect is not needed at all. And where it is not needed, it goes on functioning there too, that's the problem. A meditator uses his intellect, but he uses his intuition too—he knows that their functions are different. He uses his head, he uses his heart too.

> Your head is perfectly good if it is on your shoulders. If it is somewhere else, then it is wrong.

I used to stay in Calcutta in the house of a high-court judge. His wife told me, "You are the only person my husband has any respect for. If you say something, he will listen, otherwise he won't listen to anybody. I have tried my best but I have failed. That's why I am telling it to you."

I said, "What is the problem?"

She said, "The problem is becoming bigger and bigger every day. He remains a judge twenty-four hours. Even in the bed with me he is a judge—as if he expects me also to say 'Your Honor.' With children he behaves as if they are criminals. With everybody! We are tired. He never gets down from the bench. He carries this role continuously; he never forgets it. It has gone into his head." And she was right—I knew her husband. It is good to be a judge when you are in the court, but by the time one leaves the court . . . But he carries it home, then he starts behaving the same way with the wife, with the children, with everybody. The wife was afraid of him, the children were afraid of him. The moment he entered the house there was fear everywhere. Just a moment before, the children were happily playing, enjoying. They will suddenly stop, the wife will become serious. The house will immediately turn into a court.

This is the state of millions of people: they remain the same, they carry their office home.

Your intellect is needed. Your head has its own function, its own beauty, but it should be in its place. There are far greater things that are beyond the reach of the head, and when you are moving into those realms, you should put the head aside. You should be capable of that. That's flexibility. That is intelligence.

And remember never to get confused between intellect and intelligence. Intellect is only a part of intelligence. Intelligence is a far bigger phenomenon; it contains much more than intellect, because life is not only intellectual, life is intuitive too. Intelligence contains intuition. So many great discoveries have been made not by intellect but by intuition. In fact, all the great discoveries have been made by the intuition.

Something far deeper exists in you. You should not forget it. Intellect is only the periphery, the circumference, it is not the center of your being. The center of your being is intuition.

When you put your intellect aside, when you put your head aside, then something deeper inside you starts functioning that is incomprehensible from the periphery.

> *Some things are beyond the reach of the head, and when you are moving into those realms, you should put the head aside. You should be capable of that. That's flexibility. That is intelligence.*

Your center starts functioning, and your center is always in tune with the whole. Your circumference is your ego, your center is in tune with Tao. Your center is not yours, it is not mine; the center is universal. Circumferences are personal—your circumference is your circumference, my circumference is my circumference—but my center and your center are not two things; at the center we all meet and are one.

That's why the mystics come to know about the oneness of existence—because it depends on intuition. Science goes on dividing, splitting; it reaches to the minutest particle. The world becomes a multiplicity, it is no longer a universe.

In fact, scientists should stop using the word *universe;* they should start using a new word, *multiverse*. *Universe* has a mystical tone—*universe* means one. The mystic reaches to one; that is the experience of the center. But the center can function only when you move from the circumference to the center. It needs a quantum leap.

IMAGINATION

The faculty of intuition and the faculty of creating your own reality are absolutely not only different, but diametrically opposite things. Intuition is only a mirror. It does not create anything, it only reflects. It reflects that which is. It is pure, silent, crystal clear water reflecting the stars and the moon. It does not create anything. It is the clarity that in the East has been called the third eye. Eyes don't create anything, they simply inform you what is there.

> Intuition is only a mirror. It does not create anything, it only reflects. It reflects that which is.

Creating one's own reality is called imagination—that is the faculty of dreaming. In the night, you create so many things in your dreams. And the most amazing thing is that your whole life you have been dreaming every night, and you know every morning that it was a dream—not real. But when the night comes again, and you fall asleep and your imagination starts spreading its wings, no doubt arises in you—without any doubt you accept its reality.

This faculty of imagination can function in other ways also.

It creates your dreams—which you know are not real. But when they come, and you are surrounded by them, they appear absolutely real—more real than the real world. Because in the real world once in a while you can suspect, you can doubt. For example, this very moment you are capable of doubting whether what you are seeing here or hearing here is real, or if you have fallen asleep and you are seeing a dream. It can be a dream. You will know only when you wake up.

> In reality, you can doubt—"it could be a dream"—but in a dream you cannot wonder if it is a dream. That's the only distinction between dream and reality.

This is the only distinction: in reality, you can doubt—"it could be a dream"—but in a dream you cannot wonder if it is a dream. That's the only distinction between dream and reality. Reality allows you reason; imagination does not allow you reason.

The same faculty can create daydreams . . . you are just sitting silently, not doing anything, and a dream starts floating in your eyes; you are awake but you start thinking about being the president of the country. Because you are awake, an undercurrent knows that you are having stupid ideas; but still they are so sweet that one goes on dreaming that one has become a world conqueror, or the richest man in the world. He's awake, but he's creating a dream. If this becomes too much, you lose your sanity. You can go into any madhouse, any psychiatric hospital, and you will be surprised how people are living in their imaginations: talking to people who are not there—not only talking, but even answering from their side—and there is no doubt, no skepticism.

Imagination can create a kind of insanity if it starts believing in its own daydreams—it can create hallucinations. As far as I'm concerned, your so-called saints, great religious leaders who have seen God, who have met God, who have talked with God, are in that category. Their God is just their imagination.

There is a certain method if you want to check it. The time needed is at least three weeks, and you have to do two things to prepare the ground to create a hallucination. Then you can see Jesus Christ standing before you, or Gautam Buddha, and you can have a good chitchat. You can ask questions and you will be answered—although nobody else will see that somebody is there, but that is their fault. They don't have the spiritual height to see the invisible. Two basic things are needed: One is a three-week fast. The more hungry you are, the less your intelligence functions, because intelligence needs a certain amount of vitamins continuously—if they are not supplied, it starts getting dim. In three weeks' time it stops functioning. So the first thing is to put the intellect to sleep. That's why all

> *Imagination can create a kind of insanity if it starts believing in its own daydreams—it can create hallucinations. As far as I'm concerned, your so-called saints, great religious leaders who have seen God, who have talked with God, are in that category.*

the religions prescribe fasting as a great religious discipline. But the psychology behind it is that within three weeks your intelligence starts to go to sleep. And then imagination can function perfectly well—there is nobody to doubt.

The second requirement is aloneness—move to a place in a mountain, in a forest, in a cave, where you are absolutely alone. Because man is brought up in a society, he has always lived with people. He's talking the whole day—yakkety-yak, yakkety-yak. At night he's talking in his dreams, and from the morning he starts and goes on till he goes to sleep. If there is nobody to talk to, he starts praying to God. That is talking to God, that is a respectable way of being crazy.

Within three weeks' time . . . after the second week, he starts talking aloud. After the first week, he starts talking to himself, but he knows that nobody should hear it; otherwise, they will think him mad. But by the end of the second week that fear is gone, because intelligence is getting dull. By the second week, he starts talking aloud. By the third week, he starts seeing the person he wanted to meet: Jesus Christ, Krishna, Mahavir, Gautam Buddha, a dead friend, or anybody else. After three weeks, he's capable of visualizing the person so clearly that our ordinary reality looks pale. Hence, religions have supported both these strategies: fasting, and going into isolation. That is the way, the scientific way, to go into a hallucinatory experience.

You can create your own reality: you can live with Jesus Christ again, you can have a good conversation with Gautam Buddha, you can ask questions and you can get answers—although you will be doing both the things. But it has been found that when you ask the question, your voice will be one way, and when you answer the question, your voice will be different. Naturally, this is happening in all madhouses everywhere—people are talking to the walls.

All the history of the saints who have experienced God, talked with God, has to be researched with more psychological insight. They are not different from madmen. All their pretensions, declarations that they are the only son of God, that they are the only prophet of God, that they are the only reincarnation of God, are nothing but mad assertions.

It will be a real shock if you can realize that these people were surrounded by hallucinations; they had created their own reality around themselves. Their gods are their imagination, their messages are from their own minds, the scriptures they have left behind are manufactured by them. No book is written by God, because I have gone through all those books—they are not even worth calling good literature, what to say about their holiness? They are third-class literature, but people have worshiped them.

The whole history of man can be reduced to a single statement: it has been a history of hysteria. All these saints and sages are hysterical. Only a very few have dropped imagination, have dropped the whole mind and all its faculties—but these few have not experienced God.

Buddha never saw any God. He experienced only tremendous silence, he experienced the great joy, which remained for forty-two years after his enlightenment. His enlightenment is not a fiction, because fictions cannot last that long; dreams cannot transform a man's life. After his enlightenment, he was another man. His joy remained with him just like breathing. He does not talk about gods, he does not talk about heaven and hell, he does not talk about angels. He has not seen all these things. These things have to be created first, you have to arrange yourself in a certain situation where whatever you want to see, you can see. And if a person is dying to see Jesus Christ, is ready to do anything—fasting, isolation, going into a monastery . . .

There is a monastery in Athos, in Europe, one thousand years old—perhaps the oldest monastery in Europe. The rule of the monastery is that you only enter into it, you cannot come out of it again. And there are near about ten thousand monks inside the monastery. Only when they die . . . then their dead bodies are put through a hole, and other Christians who are outside—who are not monks—make a grave for them. But insiders cannot even come out with the dead body.

Now what are these people doing? Just chanting "Ave Maria." The monastery is dedicated to the mother of Jesus, Mary, or Maria. The whole day their only work is to go on chanting "Ave Maria." Fasting, in isolation, cut off from the world . . . soon they start hallucinating that Mother Maria visits them. They have their cells, living alone, separate from each other. They are not allowed to talk to each other, only to the abbot. In one thousand years, no woman has been allowed inside the monastery—not even a six-month-old baby. Those monks are sitting on volcanoes of repressed sexual energy.

This repressed sexual energy is also helpful in creating hallucinations. Everybody knows young men start hallucinating about girls, girls start hallucinating about boys. Their dreams become more and more sexual; sex becomes the dominant factor in their minds. And because these monks have repressed sex and are fasting, living in isolation, just thinking only of Jesus Christ or Ave Maria, naturally they start hallucinating. And those who start hallucinating become more respected, more honored. The greatest madman inside the monastery becomes the abbot.

There are many things to do to release these people from these madhouses called monasteries, nunneries, to bring them back to sanity, bring them back to the world of reality and not of dreams. You don't have to create your reality, you just have to cleanse your senses to feel the reality and its psychedelic beauty, its colorfulness, its greenness, its aliveness.

And inside, you have to discover the reality, not create it; because anything created by you cannot be but imagination. You simply have to go in, in silence, and watch—just be alert and aware so that you can see whatever is real. And those who have seen reality say you will experience tremendous silence, great joy, infinite blissfulness, immortality; but you will not see any God, and you will not see any angels. Those things have to be created to be seen.

Intuition, imagination, intellect, all have to be transcended. You have to come to a point that is beyond mind: a deep serenity, coolness, and calmness that is your true nature, that is your buddha nature. That's what you are, that is the stuff you are made of, and that is the stuff the whole universe is made of. We can call it universal consciousness, we can call it universal godliness—any name will do. But remember, millions have fooled themselves with imagination. And it is cheap, very easy—just a certain strategy has to be followed and you can create the reality.

I was once staying with a friend. In India there is a holy

festival, and on that festival people use something similar to marijuana, called bhang. The man I was staying with was a professor in a university—a very simple, good man. And I had told him, "Don't do that stupid thing." But he went to meet a few friends, and they gave him sweets that were full of marijuana, and some cold drinks that were also full of marijuana. He did not return, it was the middle of the night. I had to go to find him—what was happening? He was standing naked, surrounded by a crowd, shouting obscenities, and people were throwing stones at him.

I could not figure out what had happened. I stopped the people; I said, "I know this man. It seems he has taken some drug." Somehow, I put his clothes back on him—he was very much against it. I was pulling his pants up and he would jump out of them. And then he ran away.

The city was unknown to me, but well known to him. I followed him for a few minutes through small streets, then lost track. In the morning, the police phoned me that my friend was in their custody, so I went to the jail. By then he had come a little bit to his senses, yet there was a hangover. But he recognized me and said, "I'm sorry that I did not listen to you." He had wounds on his body because people had thrown stones.

I brought him back, and after that day the fear of police caught his mind, possessed his mind, because the police must have beaten him. Otherwise he was not going to wear his clothes, and he must have misbehaved with them. Such a fear entered, such a paranoia, that life became difficult. In the night, a policeman was guarding the street. He would hear the sound of the boots, and he would just jump under the bed. I would say, "Balram"—that was his name—"what are you doing?"

He would say, "Keep quiet. The police are coming."

I had to ask the principal to give him fifteen days' leave so he could rest, because it was so difficult to bring him to the university. Everything became suspicious—two persons would be standing by the corner of the street, talking, and he would say, "Look, they are all conspiring. And I tell you that they will finally catch hold of me, and they will put me in jail and beat me. Do something!" A police van would pass, and he would say, "My God! They have come."

I tried in every possible way to show that it was just a fear. I could understand how it had started, but now it was too much. He wouldn't listen, and neither would he sleep nor would he allow me to sleep. Finally, I had to go to a police inspector, and I told him the whole story. I told him, "You need to give me some help. This man is very simple, innocent, he has not committed any crime—he has just taken marijuana. I don't know what else was mixed in the sweets and the drinks he has taken. The police must have beaten him; otherwise, he was not going to put his clothes on. I had tried to help, but he jumped up and ran away."

The inspector said, "In what way can I help?"

I said, "You have to come with a file—because he's saying again and again, 'They have a file against me, and they are waiting for the right moment to arrest me.' So you bring any file, handcuffs, and an arrest warrant—any paper. Just seeing you, he will lose all intelligence. And come in the night, he has to be arrested at night.

"And then I will persuade you, and I will give you five thousand rupees to leave the poor guy alone. And, very reluctantly, you should let him go, and I will ask you to burn the file. So burn the file, and as you are leaving us, tell me so he can hear, 'Now there is no problem because the file is burned and there is no longer any charge in the hands of the police.' And I can take those five thousand rupees back later on."

The man was very good. He said, "I will come." He came in the night, and the moment he came my friend slipped under the bed. The inspector had to pull him out, and Balram said, "Listen, look, I have been telling you that they will come . . . and he has come, and this is the file."

The inspector gave me the arrest warrant and said, "He has to be arrested." And he put the handcuffs on Balram. I tried to persuade the inspector, but he said, "I cannot do anything. He will spend at least five years in jail."

And Balram looked at me and said, "Look, now do something; otherwise, I'm gone."

So I gave five thousand rupees to the inspector and told him, "He's a simple man. Just do me a little favor—let him go. If he does anything again, then I will be the first man to deliver him to the police. But this is his first crime, and he has committed it under the influence of a drug." With difficulty I convinced the inspector to burn the file; and we burned the file. The handcuffs were taken off and the inspector told me, "It is okay. If he does anything again, then I cannot help it. Right now, all that was reported to the police against him has been burned. Now the police have no power to arrest him." And from that day, Balram became perfectly okay.

Next day, I had to go again to the police station to get those five thousand rupees back. The man was really good. He could have refused to give the money back, but he gave it to me and asked, "How is he?"

I said, "He's perfectly okay. Now he even sees the policeman walking by and he does not care. I told him once or twice, 'That policeman is standing there.' He said, 'I don't care. The file is burned.' "

Balram had created a hallucination around himself. And the so-called religions are living in such hallucinations. You will be surprised to know that the most ancient scriptures of the Hindus talk about a certain drug, *somras,* which used to be found in the Himalayas and perhaps is still available, but we don't know how to recognize it. It was the usual practice for all religious people to drink *somras.*

One of the most intelligent men of the twentieth century, Aldous Huxley, was very much impressed when LSD was discovered—he was the first promoter of LSD. He lived under the illusion that through LSD you can achieve the same spiritual experiences that Gautam Buddha had, that Kabir had, that Nanak had. Thinking of the *somras* of the Vedas, Huxley has written in his book *Heaven and Hell* that in the future the ultimate drug will be created by science, synthetic. Its name will be in memory of the first drug used by the religious people—*somras.* Its name will be *soma.*

And since the times of the Rigveda in India, Hindu sannyasins, Hindu religious people, have been taking all kinds of drugs to experience their imaginary gods. To such a point that I have come across a follower of Kabir . . . the followers go on drinking all kinds of drugs, and a point comes when they become immune. Then they start keeping cobras and they make the cobras bite on the followers' tongues. Only that gives them the religious experience! I have seen one monastery of the followers of Kabir where they had big cobras, dangerous cobras—just one bite and you are finished, there is no cure. But those monks needed it because no other drug was effective anymore.

It is not just a coincidence that in the West the younger generation has become interested in both things together, in drugs and in the East. They come to the East to find some way to experience something beyond the ordinary, mundane world of which they have seen enough. Now sex is no longer appealing, alcohol is no longer interesting, so they start coming to the East to find some techniques to create a reality. And in most of the ashrams in the East, they will find techniques that help your imagination. They are subtle kinds of drugs.

And in the West, many have taken to drugs. Now there are thousands of young people—men and women—suffering in jails in Europe and America for taking drugs.

But as far as I'm concerned, I

> You can create a reality through drugs, but it is going to last for a few hours and then you have to take the drug again. And each time you have to take more and more quantities because you go on becoming immune.

see it in a different light. I see it as the beginning of a search for something beyond the ordinary world—although they are searching in a wrong way. Drugs won't give them the reality. You can create a reality through drugs, but it is going to last for a few hours and then you have to take the drug again. And each time you have to take more and more quantities because you go on becoming immune.

But there is a great upsurge among the younger people, which has never been seen before, of interest in drugs. They are ready to suffer imprisonment, and they come out and they are still taking drugs. In fact, if they have money, they even manage in jail to get drugs from the officers of the jail, the staff of the jail; you just have to give money to them.

But I don't see it as a bad sign. I simply see it as a misdirected young generation. The intention is right but there is nobody to tell them that drugs won't fulfill your desire and your longing. Only meditation, only silence, only transcending beyond your mind, is going to give you contentment and fulfillment.

But they cannot be condemned as they are being condemned and punished. The older generation is responsible because it doesn't have alternatives for them.

I propose the only alternative—as you become more and more meditative, you don't need anything else. You don't need to create a reality because you start seeing the reality itself. And a created reality is just false, it is a dream—maybe a sweet dream, but a dream is a dream, after all. The thirst is right, it's just that people are wandering. And their religious leaders, their political leaders, their governments, and their educational institutions are not capable of giving them a right direction.

I take it as a symptom of a great search, which has to be welcomed. Just a right direction has to be given—which the old religions cannot give, which the old society is impotent to give. We need, urgently, the birth of a new humanity. We need, urgently, to change all this sickness and ugliness that is destroying many, many people in the world.

> A created reality is just false, it is a dream—maybe a sweet dream, but a dream is a dream, after all.

Everybody needs to know himself, his reality. And it is good that the desire has arisen. Sooner or later, we will be able to turn younger people in the right direction. The people who have become sannyasins have gone through all the drug trips. And as they became sannyasins and started meditating, by and by their drugs disappeared. Now they don't need them. No punishment, no jail, just a right direction—and the reality is so fulfilling, is such a benediction, that you cannot expect more.

Existence gives you—in such abundance—richness of being, of love, of peace, of truth, that you cannot ask for more. You cannot even imagine more.

POLITICS

The world of politics is basically of the instinctive level. It belongs to the law of the jungle: might is right. And the people who get interested in politics are the most mediocre. Politics needs no other qualifications except one—that is, a deep feeling of inferiority.

Politics can be reduced almost into a mathematical maxim: Politics means will to power.

Friedrich Nietzsche has even written a book, *Will to Power*. Will to power expresses itself in many ways. So you have to understand by *politics* not only the politics that is known by the name. *Wherever* somebody is trying a power number, it is politics. It does not matter whether it relates to the state, the government, and matters like that. . . .

To me, the word *politics* is much more comprehensive than is generally understood. Man has been trying throughout history a political strategy over women—that she is lower than him. And he has convinced the woman herself. And there were reasons that the woman was helpless and had to concede to this ugly idea that is absolutely absurd. The woman is neither inferior to man nor is she superior. They are two different categories of humanity—they cannot be compared. The very comparison is idiotic, and if you start comparing, then you will be in trouble.

Why has woman been proclaimed inferior by man all over the world?—because this was the only way to keep her in bondage, to make a slave out of her. It was easier. If she was equal, then there would be trouble; she should be condi-

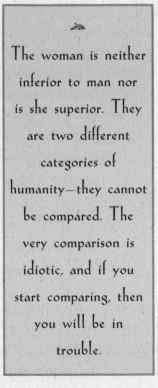

The woman is neither inferior to man nor is she superior. They are two different categories of humanity—they cannot be compared. The very comparison is idiotic, and if you start comparing, then you will be in trouble.

tioned to the idea that she is inferior. And the reasons given are that she has less muscular strength; her height is less. That she has not produced any philosophy, any theology; she has not founded any religion. That there have not been significant women artists, musicians, painters—that shows that she has not enough intelligence, she is not an intellectual. She is not concerned with higher problems of life; her concern is limited: she is only a housewife.

Now, choosing to compare this way, you can easily convince the woman that she is inferior. But this is a cunning way. There are other things also to be compared. A woman can give birth to a child, a man cannot. He is certainly inferior; he cannot become a mother. Nature has not given him that much responsibility, knowing that he is inferior. The responsibility goes to the superior. Nature has not given him a womb. In fact, his function in giving birth to a child is nothing more than that of an injection—a momentary use.

The mother has to carry the child for nine months and take all the trouble of carrying the child. It is not an easy job! And then to give birth to the child . . . that is almost as if one is passing through death. Then she brings up the child for years together—and in the past she was continually giving birth to children. What time have you left her to become a great musician, a poetess, a painter? Have you given her any time? She was constantly either pregnant or taking care of the children to whom she had given birth. She was taking care of the house, so that you were able to contemplate higher things.

Just for one day, for twenty-four hours, change your work. Let *her* contemplate, create poetry or music, and for twenty-four hours you take care of the children, of the kitchen, of the house. And then you will know who is superior! Just twenty-four hours will be enough to prove to you that to take care of so many children is just to be in a madhouse. They are not so innocent as they look. They are as naughty as you can conceive, and they are doing all kinds of mischief. They will not leave you for a single moment; they want attention continuously—perhaps that is a natural need. Attention is food.

And in just one day of cooking the food for the family and the guests, you will know that in twenty-four hours you have experienced hell, and you will forget that idea that you are superior. Because in twenty-four hours you will not think even for a single split second about theology, philosophy, religion.

You have to think from other angles too. The woman has more resistance power than man. Now that is a medically established fact. Women fall sick less than men; they live longer than men, five years longer. It is a stupid society where we have decided that the husband should be four or five years older than the wife—just to prove that the husband is more experienced, elder, to keep his superiority intact. But it is not medically right because the woman is going to live five years longer. If you think medically, then the husband should be five years younger than the wife so that they can die at almost the same time.

On the one hand the husband has to be four or five years older, and on the other hand the woman is not allowed to marry again, in almost all cultures and societies. It is a new development that she is being allowed, and that too only in very developed countries. You don't allow her to remarry so she is going to live at least ten years of widowhood. This is medically unsound—just the arithmetic is not right. Why enforce ten years of widowhood on a woman? The best way would be that the wife is five years older than the man. That would settle the whole matter. There would be no need for widowers and widows.

Now, if you think that a woman lives five years longer than a man, then who is superior? If she falls sick less, has more resistance, then who is superior? Women commit suicide 50 percent less than men. The same ratio is true of madness: 50 percent fewer women become mad than men. Now, these facts have never been considered—why?

Why do men have to commit suicide at double the rate of women? It seems to be that he has no patience with life. He is too impatient and is too desirous, expectant, and when things don't go his way, then he wants to finish himself. He gets frustrated very soon. That shows a weakness: he hasn't the courage to face the problems of life. Suicide is a cowardly step. It is escaping from problems, it is not solving them.

The woman has more problems—her problems and the problems that her man creates for her. She has double the problems and still she manages to face them courageously. And you go on saying that she is weaker. Why do twice as many men as women go mad? That simply shows that a man's intellect is not made of strong materials—he pops off anytime.

But why has it been continually insisted that the woman is inferior? It is politics. It is a power game. If you cannot become the president of a country . . . it is not easy because there is so much competition. You cannot become a messiah because it is not so easy; the moment you think of becoming a messiah, crucifixion comes to the eye.

Just the other day I saw an advertisement from some Christian mission for new recruits, with Jesus hanging on the cross; and the advertisement says, "You need guts to be a priest." Great advertisement! But that means except for Jesus . . . what about all other Christian priests? They are not priests, that advertisement is proof enough. So there has been only one priest. All these popes, and cardinals, and bishops—what are these? These are not priests . . . because when Jesus proclaimed his ideas, the cross was the answer. And when these popes go around the world, there are red carpets, warm, overwhelming welcomes from presidents of the countries, prime ministers of the countries, kings and queens—this is strange. You should not misbehave with popes and bishops—yes, it is misbehavior! You are proclaiming that he is not a priest. Crucify him—that will be the only certificate that he was a genuine Christian. Crucify as many priests as you can.

> One need not be concerned only with government, the state, and connected affairs—any power trip makes you a politician. The husband trying to be superior to the wife—it is politics.

It is not my idea, it is their idea. They publish the advertisement that "you need guts," with a picture of Jesus on the cross.

It is so simple to be a politician. One need not be concerned only with government, the state, and connected affairs—any power trip makes you a politician. The husband trying to be superior to the wife—it is politics. The wife trying to be superior to the husband—because the wife simply cannot accept the idea. Even though for millions of years she has been conditioned, she finds ways to sabotage it.

That's the whole reason why the wife goes on nagging, throws tantrums, starts crying over any small matter, makes a fuss over anything—things that you could not even have imagined would create a fuss. Why does all this happen? This is her feminine way to sabotage your political strategy: "You think you are superior? Go on thinking you are superior, and I will show you who is superior." And every husband knows who is superior; still he goes on trying to be superior. At least outside the house he straightens up, makes his tie right, smiles, and goes on as if everything is good.

In a small school, the teacher was asking the students, "Can you tell me the name of the animal who goes out of the house like a lion and comes back like a mouse?"

A small child raised his hand. The teacher said, "Yes, what is your answer?"

The child said, "My father."

Children are observant. They go on looking at what is happening. The father goes out almost like a lion, and when he comes home, he is just a mouse. Every husband is henpecked. There is no other category of husband. But why? Why has this ugly situation arisen? There is a male form of politics, there is a female form of politics—but both are trying to be on top of each other.

In every other area, for example in university: the lecturer wants to be the reader, the reader wants to be the professor, the professor wants to be the dean, the dean wants to be the vice-chancellor—a constant struggle for power. At least one would think it should not be so in education. But nobody is interested in education, everybody is interested in power.

In religion it is the same: the bishop wants to be the cardinal, the cardinal wants to be the pope. Everybody is on a ladder trying to climb higher, and others are pulling him down by the legs. Those who are higher are trying to push him so that he cannot rise up to their level. And the same is being done to those who are on a lower rung of the ladder: some are pulling on their legs, others are kicking and hitting them to keep them down as low as possible. The whole ladder, if you see it just as an observer, is a circus. And this is happening all around, everywhere.

So to me, politics means an effort to prove yourself superior. But why?—because you feel, deep down, inferior. And the man of instinct is bound to feel inferior—he *is* inferior. It is not an "inferiority complex," it is a fact, a reality—he is inferior. To live the life of instinct is to live at the lowest possible level of life.

If you understand the struggle,

> ☙
>
> Politics means an effort to prove yourself superior. But why?—because you feel, deep down, inferior. And the man of instinct is bound to feel inferior—he *is* inferior. It is not an "inferiority complex," it is a fact, a reality—he is inferior.

the fight for being superior, you drop out of the fight—you simply say, "I am myself, neither superior nor inferior." If you just stand by the side and watch the whole show, you have entered into the second world—the world of intelligence and consciousness.

It is only a question of understanding the whole rotten situation in which everybody is caught. You have just to give a little patient observation to the whole situation: "What is happening? And even if I reach to the highest rung of the ladder, what is the point?" You are just hung up in the sky looking like a fool. There is nowhere else to go.

Of course, you cannot come down because people will start joking about you: "Where are you going? What happened? Are you defeated?" You cannot come down and you cannot go anywhere else because there is no step higher, so you are hung up in the sky pretending that you have arrived, that you have found the goal of life. And you know that you have not found anything. You have simply been a fool and your whole life is wasted. Now there is no way to go up, and if you go down, then everybody is going to laugh.

So anybody who becomes a president of a country or a prime minister of a country—his only prayer is that he should die at his post. Because lower you cannot go—that is insulting, humiliating; and there is no way to go higher. You are stuck; only death can release you from the dilemma.

Man is continuously trying in every possible way to be somebody higher, special, superior—but this is all politics. And according to me, only the mediocre people are interested. The intelligent people have something more important to do. Intelligence cannot waste itself in struggling with third-class, ugly politics, dirty poli-

tics. Only the third-class people become presidents, prime ministers. An intelligent person is not going to be distracted by such a
desert, which leads nowhere, not even to an oasis.

So on the instinctive level politics is just "might is right"—the law
of the jungle. Adolf Hitler, Joseph
Stalin, Mussolini, Bonaparte, Alexander, Tamerlane—all these people
are more like wolves than human
beings. If we want a real humanity
in the world, we should cross out
these people's names completely. We
should forget that these people have
existed; they were just nightmares.
But strangely, the whole of history is
full of all these people.

What is history? Just cuttings
from newspapers of ancient times. If
you go and help somebody, no
newspaper is going to publish the
story; you go and kill somebody, and
all the newspapers are full of it. And
what is your history about except
these people who have been a nui-
sance, who have left wounds on human consciousness? This you call
history? You have only this garbage
in your mind.

> *What is history?
> Just cuttings from
> newspapers of ancient
> times. If you go and
> help somebody, no
> newspaper is going to
> publish the story; you
> go and kill somebody,
> and all the
> newspapers are full of
> it. And what is your
> history about except
> these people who
> have been a nuisance,
> who have left wounds
> on human
> consciousness?*

It is strange that the real flowers of intelligence are not even mentioned. It was so difficult for me to find out about these people. I had been looking in so many libraries, trying to find out something more about these people, who are really the creators! They have laid the foundations. But we know only one kind of world, the world where might is right.

Now on the second level, *right* is might. Intelligence believes in finding what is right.

There is no need to wrestle with swords or bombs and kill each other, because might does not prove anything right. Do you think that Muhammad Ali boxing with Gautam Buddha . . . of course Ali will be the winner in the first round. There will not be a second round, the first hit will be enough; poor Buddha will be flattened! And seeing the situation, he himself will start counting: one, two, three, four, five, six, seven, eight, nine, ten. He will not wait for the referee to count. And he will not move from the ground; lying flat on the ground, he will count up to ten. And he will say, "It is finished—you are the winner."

But might does not prove right—it is perfectly okay in the world of animals and in the world of instinct. Intelligence reverses the whole thing: "right is might"—and right has to be decided by intelligence, by logic, by reason, by argument.

That's what Socrates was doing in the court. He was ready to answer any question that the juries and the judges wanted to ask. He asked, "What are my crimes? Just start telling them one by one—I am ready to answer." They knew that it was impossible to argue with this man—but vague crimes, they thought perhaps Socrates could not answer about these. And even if he did, the jurors were not going to be convinced, because it would go against their whole conditioning. The first thing they said was, "The greatest crime that you have been committing is that you are corrupting the minds of the youth."

Socrates said, "That's true, but it is not a crime. And what you call corruption I call creation. You have corrupted those peoples' minds; now I have to destroy that corruption. And if you are right, then why don't you open a school, an academy, just as I have my school and academy? People will go to whoever is right."

Since Socrates had opened his school, all the other schools of Athens had closed, because when a man like Socrates is teaching, who can compete? In fact, all the teachers who had been running schools became students of Socrates. He was a real master. Socrates said, "You present before me a single young man who is being corrupted by me—and what do you mean by corruption?"

They said, "You teach that there is no God or gods."

He said, "Yes—because there is no God, there are no gods. What can I do about it? It is not my responsibility. If God does not exist, are you corrupting the minds of youth, or am I corrupting the minds of youth? I am simply telling the truth. Do you think truth can corrupt the minds of the youth?" The debate continued for days.

Finally the judges decided, "As far as intelligence is concerned, he has shut the mouth of you all—a single man alone against the whole mediocre society of Athens—so we should not argue anymore; we will simply ask for a vote."

Socrates said, "Voting cannot prove what is right and what is wrong. In fact, the greater possibility is that the people will vote for that which is wrong, because the majority consists of mediocre people."

Socrates was trying to establish that right should be decided by intelligence. That's what finally created the whole evolution of science. Socrates should be known as the father of all science, because in science it is not a question of "You are powerful, that's why you are right." The question is that anybody can prove to be right; how powerful you are does not matter. The question has to be decided by logic, by reason—in the lab, with experiments and experience.

So on the second level of consciousness, politics is a totally different matter.

For two thousand years India has been in slavery—for many reasons, but one of the reasons and the most fundamental reason is that all of India's intelligent people turned their backs on the politics of the lowest, the third class, the instinctive level. All in telligent people were simply not interested in politics or power. Their whole interest was to decide what is true, what is the meaning of life. Why are we here?

At the time of Gautam Buddha, perhaps all over the whole world the second level of consciousness came to its highest peak. In China, Confucius, Lao Tzu, Mencius, Chuang Tzu, Lieh Tzu— these were the people, contemporaries. In India, Gautam Buddha, Mahavira, Makhkhali Ghosal, Ajit Keshkambal, Sanjay Vilethiputta—they were overpowering, giants. In Greece, Socrates, Plato, Aristotle, Heraclitus, Pythagoras—they touched the very peak of intelligence. All over the world, suddenly it was as if a tidal wave of intelligence came. Only idiots kept fighting; all the intelligent people were deep into finding ways of deciding what is right and what is wrong.

In India it was a tradition for every philosopher to travel all over the country, challenging others. Challenge was not inimical—you have to understand that. On the second level there is no enmity; both challengers are seekers. It is a friendly phenomenon, it is not a fight; they both want the truth to win. Neither of them is trying to win over the other; that is not the question at all.

When Shankara began his discussion with Mandan Mishra, he touched his feet and asked his blessing, that truth win. Now, to touch the feet of your enemy—what does it show? There is no question of conquering the person. He is old and respected all over the country; Shankara is just a young man, thirty years old. Mandan Mishra is of his grandfather's age—Shankara touches Mandan Mishra's feet, because it is not a question of defeating him. And he asks for a blessing—not so he should be the winner but that the truth should win. And truth is nobody's property.

That was happening all over the country. And such great intellectuals were born that even today we cannot find that quality, that sharpness—for the simple reason that all the intellectuals have moved toward science. Philosophy is deserted. At that time, all those people were in the world of philosophy.

But you have to remember, it is a fight but no longer a personal quarrel—not a desire to prove oneself superior but an inquiry to find the truth. The whole emphasis has changed: it is about the victory of the true. The famous dictum in the Indian history of philosophy is *Satyameva jayate*—"Truth should win, no matter who is defeated." It is not arising out of an inferiority complex, but it is coming out of a really superior intelligence.

The tradition went to China, to Japan, and it spread to other fields also. That is why if you see two Japanese boxers, or aikido fighters, or jujitsu or judo fighters, you will be surprised—first they bow down to each other with tremendous respect. There is no question of enmity. This is one of the teachings of judo and all martial arts in Japan, that when you are fighting with somebody, it is not a question of personal enmity. If it is personal, you are already primed to be defeated because it is based in ego—you are falling to the lower level.

In the art of judo, whosoever proves the art of judo superior is the winner. It is not the person, it is the art that wins. Just as in philosophy it is the truth that wins, now it is the art that wins. Not even for a single moment should you remember yourself and your victory, because that will be the moment of your defeat.

And it has happened many times—which nobody else can understand except one who has understood the whole tradition of

> ᔕ
> This is one of the teachings of all martial arts in Japan, that when you are fighting with somebody, it is not a question of personal enmity. If it is personal, you are already primed to be defeated because it is based in ego—you are falling to a lower level.

the Eastern way. Sometimes there are two equally nonegoistic fighters; then nobody wins. The fight continues for days, the end goes on being postponed, but nobody wins. Every day they come and they bow down to each other—with great joy, with great respect. In fact they are honored by the person because he is not an ordinary person; just to fight with him is honor enough. And the fight continues. Finally the judges have to say, "Nobody can win because both are equally egoless—nobody can find the way to defeat the other."

Ego is the loophole. Ego is a kind of sleep in which you can be defeated. Just for a moment a thought can come in, and that's the end of you. The arts of judo, jujitsu, aikido—they are all similar, with only little differences, subtleties, but the basic foundation is one. And the basic foundation is that when you are fighting, you should not be there but utterly absent; then no sword can cut you.

And if you see two swordsmen fighting, you will simply be amazed. . . .

Once I had a friend, Chanchal Singh, and he had been trained in martial arts in Japan. He opened a school for martial arts, and he used to show us small things once in a while just as an entertainment. He said, "In Japan they have a certain training for the voice. If somebody attacks you with a sword and you don't have any weapon, you just make a certain sound and the sword will fall from his hand."

"It seems to be really something!" I said. "I have a wrestler friend; he does not know about swords, but just with a staff he could cut off your head." So I found the wrestler and told him about what this man had said. The wrestler said, "There is no problem. I will split open that man's head into two parts; just one hit, and that's enough."

The wrestler was strong, and when he went to hit Chanchal Singh—just as he raised his hand to hit, Chanchal Singh gave a shout, and the staff dropped from the wrestler's hand as if his heart had stopped beating! Whatever happened, his hand lost all its power—just the sound!

I said, "How do you make that sound?"

Chanchal Singh said, "The sound can be learned easily; the thing behind it is that you should not be there. That is the most difficult thing. I have been in Japan for all these years: everything is simple, only that is the trouble—that you should not be there. And at a time when somebody is going to make two parts of your skull, at such a time you are absolutely needed there! But even at such a time you are not to be there—only the sound, with no ego behind it. Suddenly the man will forget what he is doing, he will be completely at a loss. Even his memory for a moment has slipped. He is not aware of what is happening, of what he is doing, of what he was doing. It will take a little time for him to recover. Just your ego has to be absent. That absence creates a certain change in the mind of the person, a certain kind of break, a sudden break."

But if both persons are egoless, then it is difficult. Then a strange thing is known to happen in Japan, an everyday thing: before you take up your sword to hit the other man, the other man's sword is already ready to defend. It is not taken up after your move, no, but before you have even thought of the move.

It is as if in that split second when you think of the move, before your hand makes the move, the thought has reached the man and he is ready to defend.

That too happens only if you are absent. Then the sword is not separate from you. You are not doing anything; you are simply there, absent, allowing things to happen. But if both are egoless, then it can go on for days. Nobody can hit or even scratch the other person.

This is not the ordinary, instinctive level. You have moved to a higher level—even higher than the second. You have moved to the third level, the intuitive. Just as it can happen with swords or boxing or Eastern-style wrestling, the same can happen with intelligence on the third plane.

I have loved only two professors in my whole career. I have troubled many, and I have not left even these two alone, but I loved them. One of them was Professor S. S. Roy. He had written his doctoral thesis on Shankara and Bradley—a comparative study. He presented the first copy of it to me. I said, "This does not look good: I am your student and you are presenting me with the first copy of your thesis, as it came from the press."

He said, "In my opinion, you deserve it."

I said, "But in my opinion your whole thesis is wrong—even the title is wrong because you are comparing two men of two different levels."

Bradley is an intellectual, a great intellectual. He dominated, in the beginning part of the twentieth century, the whole world of philosophy. He was the top intellectual. Shankara is not an intellectual at all.

I said to Professor Roy, "Of course they both come to similar conclusions, that's why you have compared them; you see the conclusions are similar. But you don't see that they come to similar conclusions from different routes. And that's my objection to it— because Bradley simply comes to those conclusions through logic, while Shankara comes to those conclusions through experience.

"Shankara is not just arguing about them as a philosopher. He argues as a philosopher too, but that is secondary. He has experienced a truth. Now, to express that truth he uses logic, reason, intellect. Bradley has no experience—and he admits that he has no experience, but intellectually he finds these conclusions the most tenable, the most valid."

So I told Professor Roy, "If you ask me, you have compared two totally different persons who are not comparable."

And there were other points, but that basic point was continually coming up, again and again. It is possible to come to a conclusion just logically, and it may be right, may not be right; you cannot be certain about its rightness. But to Shankara it is not a question of whether it may be right or not: it is right. Even if you prove logically that he is wrong, he will not move from his position. Bradley will—if you can prove to him that he is wrong, he will move.

I said, "Shankara and Bradley both are saying that God, Brahma, truth, is absolute. But the difference is that Bradley will change his standpoint if you make a logical argument against him and prove the flaws in his argument. Shankara will simply laugh and say, 'You are right. My way of expressing it was wrong, and I knew that somebody who knows the truth will find that the expression is wrong. You are absolutely right, my expression is wrong.' But Shankara will not concede that he is wrong. His position is that of experience, it is intuitive."

There is no fight at all at the intuitive level.

The politician on the instinct level is just a wild animal. He does not believe in anything except being victorious. Whatever means are needed to be victorious, he will use. The end justifies all his means, howsoever ugly they are. Adolf Hitler says in his autobiography, "Means don't matter; what matters is the end. If you succeed, whatever you have done is right; if you fail, whatever you have done is wrong. You lie, but if you succeed, it will become truth. Do anything, just keep in mind that success must be at the end. Then success, retroactively, makes everything right. And defeat . . . you may go on doing everything right, but defeat will prove everything wrong."

On the second level there is a struggle, but now the struggle is human; it is of intellect.

Yes, there is still a certain struggle to prove that what you are holding to is true, but the truth is more important than you. If you are defeated in favor of greater truth, you will be happy, not unhappy. When Shankara defeated Mandan Mishra, Mandan Mishra immediately stood up, touched the feet of Shankara, and asked to be initiated as his disciple. There is no question of fight. It is a human, far superior world of intelligence.

But still, somewhere in the name of truth, a little politics is lurking behind the scenes. Otherwise, what is the need even to challenge this man? If you know the truth, enjoy it! What is the point of going around the whole country defeating people? If you know the truth, people will come to you. There are some subtle politics in it. You can call it philosophical politics, religious politics, but it is still politics, very refined.

Only on the third level, when intuition starts functioning, is there no fight at all. Buddha never went to anybody to conquer them, Mahavira never went to anybody to conquer them, Lao Tzu never went to anybody to conquer them. People came; whoever was thirsty came to them. They were not even interested in those who came to challenge them for an intellectual discussion.

Many came—Sariputta came, Moggalayan came, Mahakashyap came—to Buddha. All these people were great philosophers with thousands of disciples, and they came to challenge Buddha. His simple process throughout his whole life was, "If you know, I am happy. You can consider yourself to be victorious. But do you know? I know, and I don't think that I have to challenge anybody. Because there are only two types of people—those who know and those who don't know. Those who don't know, how can I challenge those poor fellows? It is out of the question. Those who know—how can I challenge those rich fellows? That is out of the question."

Buddha asked Sariputta, "If you know, I am happy—but do you know? And I am not challenging you, simply inquiring. Who are you? If you don't know, then drop the idea of challenging me. Then just be here with me. Someday, in some right moment, it may happen—not through challenge, not though discussion, not even through expression."

And people were really honest. Sariputta bowed down and said, "Please forgive me for challenging you. I *don't* know. I am a skillful arguer and I have defeated many philosophers, but I can see you are not a philosopher. And now the time has come for me to

> In a better world the people of intuition will be the guiding lights for those who can understand them intellectually. And the intellectual politicians—professors, the intelligentsia, theoreticians—will be the guide for the instinctive politicians. Only this way can the world be at ease.

surrender and to see from this new angle. What am I supposed to do?"

Buddha said, "You have just to be silent for two years." That was a simple process for every challenger who came—and many came: "Two years' complete silence and then you can ask any question." And two years' silence is enough, more than enough. After two years they have even forgotten their own names, they have forgotten all challenge, all idea of victory. They have tasted the man. They have tasted his truth.

So on the intuitive level there is no politics at all.

In a better world the people of intuition will be the guiding lights for those who can at least understand them intellectually. And the intellectual politicians—professors of politics, the intelligentsia, theoreticians—they will be the guide for the instinctive politicians. Only this way can the world be at ease, live at ease.

The light should come from the highest level. It will have to be passed through the second category, because only then may the third category be able to catch hold of something of it; the second category will function as a bridge. That's how it was in ancient India.

It happened once. . . .

The really intuitive people lived in the forests or in the mountains, and the intellectuals—the professors, the pundits, the scholars, the prime ministers—used to come to them with their problems because, they said, "We are blind—you have eyes." It happened to Buddha. He was conducting his camp by the side of a river, and on both sides armies were standing. There were two kingdoms and the river was the boundary, and they had been fighting for generations over which kingdom the river belonged to, because the water was valuable. And they had not been able to decide—so many times they had made the river red with blood and the fight had continued.

Buddha had his camp there and the generals of both the armies came to him. Just by chance, they each entered his camp at the same time and saw each other. They were shocked at this strange coincidence, but now there was no way to go back. Buddha said, "Don't be worried; it is good that you have come together. You both are blind, your predecessors have been blind. The river goes on flowing, and you go on killing people. Can't you see a simple fact? You both need water, and the river is big enough.

"There is no need to possess the river—and who can be the possessor? All the water is flowing into the ocean. Why can't both of you use it? One side belongs to one kingdom, the other side belongs to the other kingdom—there is no problem. And there is no need even to draw a line in the middle of the river because lines cannot be drawn on water. Use the water, rather than fighting."

It was so simple. And they understood that their fields and their crops were dying because they had no one to care for them.

Fighting was first: Who possesses the river? First the water had to be possessed; only then could you water all your fields.

But the stupid mind thinks only in terms of possession. The man of insight thinks of utility.

Buddha simply said, "Use it! And come to me again when you have used all the water. Then there will be a problem, and then we will see. But come to me again only when you have used all the water."

The water is still flowing after twenty-five centuries. How can you use all the water? It is a big river, thousands of miles long. It brings the water from the eternal snows of the Himalayas and takes it to the Bay of Bengal. How can you exhaust it? And those kingdoms were just small kingdoms. Even if they wanted to exhaust it, there was no way.

The insight should come from the intuitive person. But the insight can only be understood by the intelligent, and the intelligent can help the politicians of instinct, for whom the only desire is power.

This I call meritocracy because the ultimate merit dominates and influences the lower rungs and helps them to rise above their level. It has no vested interest, and because it has no vested interest, it is free and its insight is clear. It will be difficult for the intuitive person to explain anything to the instinctive person because they are so far apart, belonging to two different dimensions without any bridge. In the middle, the intellectual can be of immense help.

The universities, the colleges, the schools, should not only teach political science—it is such a stupid idea to teach political science! Teach political science but also teach political art, because science is of no use; you have to teach practical politics. And those professors in the universities should prepare politicians, give them certain qualities. Then the people who are ruling now all over the world will be nowhere at all. Then you will find rulers well trained, cultured, knowing the art and the science of politics, and always ready to go to the professors, to the scholars. And slowly it may be possible that they can approach the highest level of meritocracy: the intuitive people.

If this is possible, then we will have, for the first time, something that is really human—giving dignity to humanity, integrity to individuals.

For the first time you will have some real democracy in the world. What exists now as democracy is not democracy—it is mobocracy.

STRATEGIES

❦

Drop the mind that thinks in prose;
revive another kind of mind that thinks in poetry.
Put aside all your expertise in syllogism;
let songs be your way of life.
Move from intellect to intuition,
from the head to the heart,
because the heart is closer to the mysteries.

PEEL THE ONION

Man's being is simple, but his personality is not; the personality is complex. The personality is like an onion—there are many layers of conditioning and corruption, and hidden behind those many layers is man's simple being. It is behind so many filters that you cannot see it—and hidden behind these many filters, you cannot see the world either, because whatsoever reaches you is corrupted by the filters before it reaches you.

Nothing ever reaches you as it is; you go on missing it. There are many interpreters in between. You see something—first your eyes and your senses falsify it. Then your ideology, your religion,

your society, your church—they falsify it. Then your emotions—
they falsify it. And so on, and so forth . . . By the time it reaches
to you, it has almost nothing of the original, or so little that it
makes no difference. You see something only if your filters allow
it, and the filters don't allow much.

Scientists agree; scientists say we see only 2 percent of reality—
only 2 percent! Ninety-eight percent is missed. When you are
listening to me, you will hear only 2 percent of what has been
said. Ninety-eight percent will be lost, and when the 98 percent
is lost, that 2 percent is out of context. It is as if you have taken
two pages from a novel at random, one from here, one from there,
and then you start reconstructing the whole novel from these two
pages. Ninety-eight pages are missing! You have no inkling what
they were; you don't even know that they existed. You have only
two pages and you reconstruct the whole novel again. This re-
construction is your invention. It is not a discovery of truth, it is
your imagination.

And there is an inner necessity to fill the gaps. Whenever you
see that two things are unrelated, the mind has an inner urgency
to relate them; otherwise it feels uneasy. So you invent a link. You
fix those loose things with a link, you bridge them, and you go
on inventing a world that is not there.

George Gurdjieff used to call these filters "buffers." They protect you against reality. They protect your lies, they protect your
dreams, they protect your projections. They don't allow you to
come into contact with reality because the very contact is going
to be shattering, shocking. Man lives through lies.

Friedrich Nietzsche is reported to have said, "Please don't take
the lies away from humanity, otherwise man will not be able to

live. Man lives through lies. Don't take the fictions away, don't destroy the myths. Don't tell the truth because man cannot live by truth." And he is right about 99.9 percent of people—but what kind of life can there be through lies? It will be a big lie itself. And what kind of happiness is possible through lies? There is no possibility; hence humanity is in misery. With truth is bliss; with lies there is only misery and nothing else. But we go on protecting those lies.

Those lies are comfortable, but they keep you protected against bliss, against truth, against existence.

Man is exactly like an onion. And the art consists of how to peel the onion and come to its innermost core.

> ☙
>
> Your physical senses have been trained. You see things if your society allows you to see them, you hear things if your society allows you to hear them. You touch things if your society allows you to touch them.

1. THE PHYSICAL SENSES. The first layer is made of corrupted physical senses. Never for a single moment think that your physical senses are as they should be—they are not. They have been trained. You see things if your society allows you to see them, you hear things if your society allows you to hear them. You touch things if your society allows you to touch them.

Man has lost many of his senses—for example, smell. Man has almost lost the sense of smell. Just look at a dog and his capacity to smell—how sensitive is his nose!

Man seems to be very poor. What has happened to man's nose? Why can't he smell as deeply as a dog, or as a horse? The horse can smell for miles. The dog has an immense memory of smells; man has no memory. Something is blocking the nose.

Those who have been looking deeply into these layers say that it is because of the repression of sex that the sense of smell is lost. Physically, man is as sensitive as any other animal—but psychologically his nose has been corrupted. Smell is one of the most sexual doors into your body. Through smell, animals start feeling whether a male is in tune with the female or not; the smell is a subtle hint. When the female is ready to make love to the male, she releases a certain kind of smell. Only through that smell does the male understand that he is acceptable. If that smell is not released, the male moves away; he knows he is not accepted.

Man has destroyed the sense of smell because it will be difficult to create a so-called cultured society if your sense of smell remains natural. You are moving on the road and a woman starts releasing her scent and gives you a signal of acceptance. She is somebody else's wife; her husband is with her—the signal is there that you are acceptable. What will you do? It will be awkward, embarrassing! Your wife is walking with you and there is no scent from her body, and suddenly a man passes by and she gives the signal—and those are unconscious signals; you cannot suddenly control them. Then you will become aware that she is interested in the other man, that she is welcoming the other man. That will create trouble! So down the centuries, man has destroyed his sense of smell completely.

It is not just accidental that in cultured countries much time is wasted in removing all kinds of smell from the body. The body odor has to be completely destroyed by deodorants, deodorant soaps. It has to be covered by layers of perfume, strong perfume. These are all disguises; these are ways to avoid a reality that is still there. Smell is very sexual, that's why we have destroyed the nose, utterly destroyed the nose.

Even in language you can see the difference. To see means one thing; to hear, one thing; but to "smell" means just the opposite. To see means a capacity to see, but to smell does not mean the capacity to smell. It means that you are "smelly." Even in language the repression has entered.

And the same has happened with other senses. You don't look at people eye to eye—or, if you do look at them, it is only for a few seconds. You don't look at people really; you go on avoiding. If you look, it is thought to be offensive. Just be aware: Do you really see people, or do you go on avoiding their eyes?—because if you don't avoid them, then you may be able to see a few things that the person is not willing to show. It is not good manners to see something that he is not willing to show, so it is better to avoid.

We listen to the words, we don't see the face—because many times the words and the face are contradictory. A man is saying one thing and he is showing another. Gradually we have completely lost the ability to see the face, the eyes, the gestures. We only listen to the words. Just watch this, and you will be surprised how people go on saying one thing and showing another. And nobody detects it because you have been trained not to look directly into the face. Or, even if you look, the look is not that of awareness, not that of attention. It is empty; it is almost as if you are not looking.

We hear sounds by choice. We don't hear all kinds of sounds. We choose—whatsoever is useful we hear. And to different societies and different countries, different things are valuable. A man who lives in a primitive world, in a forest, in a jungle, has a different kind of receptivity for sounds. He has to be continuously alert and aware of the animals; his life is in danger. You need not be alert; you live in a cultured world where animals don't exist anymore and there is no fear. Your survival is not at stake. Your ears don't function perfectly because there is no need.

People go on saying one thing and showing another. And nobody detects it because you have been trained not to look directly into the face. Or, even if you look, the look is not that of awareness, not that of attention.

Have you seen a hare or a deer? How attentive they are, how sensitive. Just a small sound—a dead leaf stirred by the wind—and the deer is alert. You would not have noticed it at all. And great music surrounds life, subtle music surrounds life, but we are absolutely unaware of it. There is great rhythm—but to feel it you will need more alert ears, more alert eyes, a more alert touch.

So the first layer is of corrupted physical senses. We see only what we want to see. Our whole body mechanism is poisoned. Our body has been made rigid. We live in a kind of frozenness; we are cold, closed, unavailable. We are so afraid of life that we have killed all kinds of possibilities through which life can make contact with us.

People don't touch each other, they don't hold hands, they don't hug each other. And when you hold somebody's hand, you feel embarrassed, he feels embarrassed. Even if you hug somebody, it feels as if something wrong is happening, and you are in a hurry to get away from the other's body. Because the other's body can open you—the warmth of the other's body can open you. Even children are not allowed to hug their parents; there is great fear. And all fear is basically, deep down, rooted in the fear of sex. There is a taboo against sex. A mother cannot hug her son because the son may get sexually aroused—that is the fear. A father cannot hug his daughter, he is afraid he may get physically aroused— warmth has its own ways of working. Nothing is wrong in being physically aroused or sexually aroused; it is simply a sign that one is alive, that one is immensely alive. But the fear, the sex taboo, says, "Keep away, keep a distance."

All our senses are corrupted. We have not been allowed to be natural—hence man has lost dignity, innocence, grace, elegance. This is the first layer.

And because of all these repressions the body has become non-orgasmic. There is no joy—it has happened both to man and woman in almost the same way, but man has gone deeper into corruption than woman because man is perfectionistic, neuroti- cally perfectionistic. Once he gets an idea, he tries to go to the very extreme of it. Women are more practical, less perfectionistic, less neurotic, more earthly, more balanced, less intellectual, more intuitive. They have not gone to the very end. It is good that women have not become as neurotic as men—that's why they still retain some dignity, some grace, some roundness of being, some poetry. But both have been corrupted by the society, both have become hard. Men more, women a little less, but the difference is only of degrees.

Because of this layer, everything that enters you has to pass this filter first. And this filter destroys, interprets, manipulates, gives new colors of its own, projects, invents—and the reality becomes garbed. When this layer disappears . . . That is the whole effort of yoga: to make your body alive, sensitive, young again, to give your senses their maximum functioning. Then one functions with no taboos around; then lucidity, grace, beauty, flow. Warmth arises again, openness, and growth happens. One is constantly new, young, and one is always on an adventure. The body becomes orgasmic. Joy surrounds you.

Through joy the first corruption disappears. Hence my insistence to be joyous, to be celebrating, to enjoy life, to accept the body—not only to accept it but to feel grateful that existence has given you such a beautiful body. Such a sensitive body, with so many doors to relate to reality: eyes and ears and nose and touch— open all these windows and let life's breeze flow in, let life's sun shine in. Learn to be more sensitive. Use every opportunity to be sensitive so that the first filter is dropped.

If you are sitting on the grass, don't go on pulling it up and destroying it. I had to stop sitting on the lawn—I used to meet with people on the lawn—because people would go on destroying the grass, they would go on pulling on the grass. I had to stop it. People are so violent, so unconsciously violent, they don't know what they are doing. And they were told again and again, but within minutes they would forget. They were so restless they didn't know what

> ᪥
>
> There are millions of opportunities to make your body alive again. And only you can do it. Society has done its work of corruption, you will have to undo it.

they were doing. The grass was available to their restlessness, so they would start pulling it up and destroying it.

When you are sitting on the grass, close your eyes, become the grass—be grassy. Feel that you are grass, feel the greenness of the grass, feel the wetness of the grass. Feel the subtle smell that goes on being released by the grass. Feel the dewdrops on the grass, feel that they are on you. Feel the sun rays playing on the grass. For a moment be lost into it and you will have a new sense of your body. And do it in all kinds of situations: in a river, in a swimming pool, lying on the beach in the sun rays, looking at the moon in the night, lying down with closed eyes on the sand and feeling the sand. Millions of opportunities are there to make your body alive again. And only you can do it. Society has done its work of corruption, you will have to undo it.

And once you start hearing, seeing, touching, smelling, then you smell the reality.

2. CONDITIONING. The second layer is of conditioning—social, political, religious, ideological—belief systems. Belief systems make you noncommunicative. If you are a Hindu and I am a Mohammedan, immediately there is no communication. If you are a man and I am a man, there is communication, but if you are a com-

munist and I am a fascist, communication stops. All belief systems are destructive to communication. And the whole of life is nothing *but* communicating—communicating with trees, communicating with rivers, communicating with sun and moon, communicating with people and animals. It is communication; life is communication.

Dialogue disappears when you are burdened with belief systems. How can you really be in a dialogue? You are already too full of your ideas and you think they are absolutely true. When you are listening to the other, you are just being polite; otherwise you don't listen. You know what is right, you are simply waiting until this man finishes and then you jump upon him. Yes, there can be a debate and a discussion and argumentation, but there can be no dialogue. Between two beliefs there is no possibility of dialogue. Beliefs destroy friendship, beliefs destroy humanity, beliefs destroy communion.

So if you want to see and hear and listen, then you will have to drop all belief systems. You can't be a Hindu, you can't be a Mohammedan, you can't be a Christian. You can't afford these kinds of nonsense; you have to be sensible enough to be without beliefs. Caged in your own system, you are unavailable and the other is unavailable to you.

People are moving like windowless houses. Yes, you come close, sometimes you clash with each other—but you never meet. Yes, sometimes you touch, but you never meet. You talk, but you never communicate. Everybody is imprisoned in his own conditionings; everybody is carrying his own prison around him. This has to be dropped.

Beliefs create a kind of smugness, and beliefs stop exploration

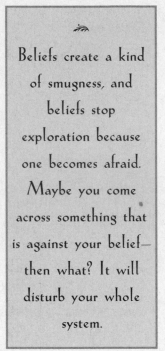

Beliefs create a kind of smugness, and beliefs stop exploration because one becomes afraid. Maybe you come across something that is against your belief—then what? It will disturb your whole system.

because one becomes afraid. Maybe you come across something that is against your belief—then what? It will disturb your whole system. So it is better not to explore—remain confined to a dull, dead, defined world; never go beyond it.

It gives you an "as if" kind of knowledge, *as if* you know. You don't know anything—you don't know anything about God, but you have a certain belief about God; you don't know anything about truth, but you have a theory about truth. This "as if" is dangerous. This is a kind of hypnotized state of the mind.

Men and women, all have been conditioned, although in different ways. Man has been conditioned to be aggressive, to be competitive, to be manipulative, to be egoistic. Man has been prepared for a different kind of work: to be the exploiter, to be the oppressor, and to be the master. Women have been given belief systems to be the slaves. They have been taught how to submit; they have been given a very, very small world, the household. Their whole life has been taken away from them. But once the belief system settles in, the woman accepts it and remains confined to it, and the man accepts his belief system and remains confined to it.

Men have been taught not to cry; tears are not manly, so men don't cry. Now what kind of foolishness is this? Crying and weeping sometimes has such a therapeutic effect—it is needed, it is a must, it unburdens. Man goes on burdening himself because he cannot cry and cannot weep, it is "unmanly." And women have been taught to cry and weep, it is perfectly womanly, so they go on crying and weeping even where it is not needed. It is just a belief system—they use it as a strategy to manipulate. The woman knows that through argument she will not be able to win over the husband, but she can cry—that works, so that becomes her argument. Man is corrupted in one way, he cannot cry, and the woman is corrupted in another way, she starts crying and uses crying as a strategy to dominate. Crying becomes political, and when your tears are political, they lose beauty; they are ugly.

> Man goes on burdening himself because he cannot cry and cannot weep, it is "unmanly." And women have been taught to cry and weep, it is perfectly womanly, so they go on crying and weeping even where it is not needed.

This second conditioning is one of the most difficult things to get rid of. It is complex. You have a certain political ideology, a certain religious ideology, and thousands of other things jumbled together in your mind. They have become so much a part of you that you don't think they are separate from you. When you say, "I am a Hindu," you don't say, "I have a belief called Hinduism," no. You say, "I am a Hindu." You are identified with Hinduism. If Hinduism is in danger, you think you are in danger. If somebody burns a temple, you think you are in danger. Or, if you are a

> You don't say, "I have a belief called Hinduism," no. You say, "I am a Hindu." You are identified with Hinduism. If Hinduism is in danger, you think you are in danger.

Mohammedan, you think you are in danger because somebody burns the Koran.

These belief systems have to be dropped. Then understanding arises; then readiness to explore, then innocence, arises. Then you are surrounded by a sense of mystery, awe, wonder. Then life is no longer a known thing, it is an adventure. It is so mysterious that you can go on exploring; there is no end to it. And you never create any belief, you remain in a state of not-knowing. On that not-knowing state Sufis insist very much, and so do Zen masters.

Remain constantly in the state of not-knowing. If you happen to know something, don't make a belief out of it. Go on dropping it, go on throwing it. Don't let it surround you, otherwise sooner or later it will become a hard crust and you will not be available again to life.

Remain always childlike—then communication becomes possible, then dialogue becomes possible. When two people who are in a state of not-knowing talk, there is meeting—they commune. There is nothing to hinder. You will be able to understand me only if you are in a state of not-knowing, because I am in that state continuously. With me, communion is possible if you drop your belief systems, otherwise they will hinder the path.

3. RATIONALIZATION. The third filter, the third layer, is pseudoreasoning, rationalization, explanations, excuses. All are borrowed. Not a single one is your own authentic experience, but they give a kind of satisfaction: you think you are a very rational being.

You cannot become rational by accumulating borrowed arguments and proofs. The real reason arises only when you are intelligent—and remember, there is a difference between an intellectual and the man whom I call intelligent. The intellectual is hidden behind the pseudoreasoning. His reasoning may be logical, but it can never be reasonable. His reason is just pseudo, it appears like reason.

Listen, I have heard:

The man was drowning. "Help, I can't swim! I can't swim!" he cried.

"I can't either," said the old man sitting on the riverbank chewing tobacco. "But I'm not hollerin' about it!"

Now this is perfectly rational: "Why are you hollerin' about it? You can't swim, neither can I, so keep quiet." But you are sitting on the bank and he is in the river; the situation is different, the context is different.

When Buddha says something, you can repeat the same thing, but the context is different. When Mohammed says something, you can repeat exactly the same thing. But

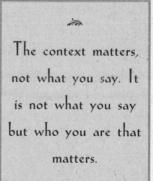

The context matters, not what you say. It is not what you say but who you are that matters.

it will not mean the same thing, because the context is different. And the context matters, not what you say. It is not what you say but who you are that matters.

I have heard:

Donnegan sat in the confessional. "Father," he moaned, "I have done something so bad, you are going to throw me out of the church."

"What did you do, my son?" asked the priest.

"Yesterday," said Donnegan, "I saw my wife sashaying in front of me and it got me so excited I grabbed her, ripped off her clothes, threw her down on the floor, and we had sex right then and there."

"That is a little unusual," said the priest, "but no reason for excommunication."

"Are you sure you're not going to throw me out of the church?"

"Of course not."

"Well," said Donnegan, "they threw us out of the supermarket!"

It all depends on the context—who you are, where you are. It depends from what point of view, from what experience you speak. I use the same words that you use, but they don't mean the same—they can't mean the same. When I utter them, I utter them; when you utter them, you utter them. The words are the same, but because they come from different spaces, they carry a different meaning, a different connotation, different flavors, a different music.

The pseudoreasoning is just apparent reasoning, it is not *knowing*. It is more for the sake of finding excuses; it is more for the sake of argumentation. In this kind of deception the male mind is expert. This is the male mind's expertise. Men have learned the art deeply. This filter is very, very strong in the male mind.

Real reasoning arises only when pseudoreasoning has been dropped.

What is real reason? Karl Jaspers has defined it perfectly. He says: Reason is openness, reason is clarity, reason is the will to unity. Reason uses logic and its methods and categories of understanding just to transcend them. Reason is the ultimate flowering of wisdom.

> Reason is openness, reason is clarity, reason is the will to unity. Reason uses logic and its methods and categories of understanding just to transcend them.

But not pseudoreasoning—beware of the pseudo. The pseudo always creates a filter, and the real always becomes a door. The real is always a bridge, and the pseudo is always a block.

This third, pseudoreasoning layer is one of the greatest disturbances in your being.

4. SENTIMENTALITY. The fourth layer is emotionality, sentimentalism. It is pseudofeeling, much ado about nothing, much fuss. The female mind is expert at this. It is kind of empty; it is just on the surface. It is impotent sympathy; it does not do a thing. If somebody is ill, you sit by their side and you cry. Your crying is

not going to help. The house is on fire and you cry—that is not going to help either. This pseudo kind of feeling has to be detected; otherwise you will never know what real feeling is.

> Whenever you really feel something in your heart, it immediately transforms you, it becomes action. That is the criterion—your feeling becomes action.

The real feeling is involvement, commitment. It is empathy, not only sympathy. It is action. Whenever you really feel something in your heart, it immediately transforms you; it becomes action. That is the criterion—your feeling becomes action. If your feeling just remains a feeling and never becomes an action, then know well that it is pseudo. Then you are deceiving yourself or somebody else.

One can never go against one's heart. If you are still going against your heart, then you must have a pseudoheart—a pretender. Just as the third layer is the field for male expertise, the fourth is the field for female expertise.

5. REPRESSION. The fifth layer is corrupted, poisoned instincts—repression.

Gurdjieff used to say that all your centers are overlapping each other, are misplaced, are interfering with each other, are trespassing, and you don't know what is what. Each center in its own functioning is beautiful, but when it starts interfering into somebody else's functioning, then there is great difficulty. Then the whole system goes neurotic.

For example, if your sex center functions as a sex center, it is perfectly good. But people have been repressing it so much that in many people the sex center does not exist in their genitals, it has moved into the head. This is what overlapping is. Now they make love through their head—hence the great importance of pornography, visualization. Even while making love to your woman, you may be thinking of some beautiful actress, that you are making love to her. Only then, suddenly you become interested in making love to your woman. In fact, your own woman is nonexistent. It is a kind of masturbation. You are not making love to her, you are making love to somebody else who is not there. You go on fantasizing in the head.

> ❧
>
> If your sex center functions as a sex center, it is perfectly good. But people have been repressing it so much that in many people the sex center does not exist in their genitals, it has moved into the head.

Religious repression has disturbed all your centers. It is difficult even to see that your centers are separate. And, each functioning in its own field, each center is perfectly right. When it interferes with another field, then problems arise. Then there is a confusion of your totality. Then you don't know what is what.

Sex can be transformed when it is confined to its own center; it cannot be transformed from the head. It has created a pseudo-center in the head.

I have heard:

From time to time, saints are allowed to visit the earth in disguise. Saint Teresa had long wanted to pay a visit to Hollywood, but Gabriel, who was in charge of the roster, thought that even a saint would not be able to come through unscathed after visiting the movie capital.

Eventually, however, Saint Teresa persuaded Gabriel that no harm would come to her, and she set off on the first available earth-bound cloud.

The weeks stretched into months without any word from earth, so one day a very worried Gabriel put through a telephone call to Los Angeles. The connection was made, the phone rang, and finally a voice said, "Terry here—who is this? . . . Gabby darling! How absolutely marvelous to hear from you!"

Your so-called saints are only avoiding the world. They are repressed beings. If opportunities are made available to them, they will fall far lower than you. They are just somehow holding themselves back because of the fear of hell and the greed for heaven. But whatsoever you have repressed because of fear or greed remains there. It not only remains there, it becomes unnatural, perverted, moves into deeper realms of your consciousness and unconsciousness. And then it becomes difficult to uproot it.

Gurdjieff was a Sufi. His whole teaching comes from Sufi masters. He introduced methods into the Western world for delineating each center and allowing each center to function in its own field.

The head should function as far as reason is concerned, that's all. Have you watched? Sometimes people say, "I think I love you." I *think* I love you? Love has nothing to do with thinking. How can you *think* that you love me? But these people don't know how to function from the heart directly; even the heart has to go via the head. They cannot simply say, "I love you."

When you speak from the heart, no language is needed. When you speak from the head, *only* language can say something; there is no other way to say it.

Watch and observe. Let the head function as reason, let the heart function as feeling, let the sex center function as sex. Let everything function in its own way. Don't allow the different mechanisms to mix into each other, otherwise you will have corrupted instincts.

When instinct is natural, untabooed, spontaneous, without any inhibition, there is a clarity in your body, a harmony in your body. There is a humming sound in your organism.

The fifth layer of repression is also the male expertise.

6. CORRUPTED INTUITION. The sixth layer is corrupted intuition.

We have become almost unaware of the phenomenon called intuition. We don't know that anything like intuition exists—because intuition is the sixth layer. Those five layers are so thick that one never comes to feel the sixth.

Intuition is a totally different kind of phenomenon from reason. Reason argues; reason uses a process to reach a conclusion. Intuition jumps—it is a quantum leap. It knows no process. It simply reaches to the conclusion without any process.

Many mathematicians have been able to do any kind of mathematical problem without going into its process. Their functioning was intuitive. You just say the problem, and before you have even said it, the conclusion will come. There has not been a time gap at all. You were saying it and the moment you finished, or even before you finished, the conclusion has come. Mathematicians have always been puzzled by these freak phenomena. These people—how do they do it? If a mathematician was to do this problem, it might take three hours or two hours or one hour. Even a computer will take at least a few minutes to do it, but these people don't take a single moment. You say it, and instantly . . . So in mathematics, intuition is now a recognized fact.

When reason fails, only intuition can work. And all the great scientists have become aware of it, that all their great discoveries are made not by reason but by intuition. Madame Curie was working for three years upon a certain problem and was trying to solve it from many directions. Every direction failed. One night, utterly exhausted, she went to sleep and she decided . . . The incident is almost like what happened to Buddha. That night she decided, "Now it is enough. I have wasted three years. It seems to be a futile search. I have to drop it." That night she dropped it and went to sleep.

> When reason fails, only intuition can work. And all the great scientists have become aware of it, that all their great discoveries are made not by reason but by intuition.

In the night she got up in her sleep; she went to her table and wrote the answer. Then she went back and fell into bed. In the morning she could not even remember, but the answer was there on the table. And nobody else had been in the room, and even if there had been somebody, the answer would not have been possible. She had been working for three years—one of the greatest minds of this age. But there was nobody and the answer was there. Then she looked more minutely: it was her handwriting! Then suddenly the dream surfaced. She remembered it as if she had had a dream in the night in which she was sitting at the table and writing something. Then by and by, everything surfaced. She had come to the conclusion from some other door, which was not reason. It was intuition.

Buddha struggled for six years to attain enlightenment but could not. One day he dropped the whole idea of attaining. He rested under a tree, and by the morning it had happened. When he opened his eyes, he was in *samadhi*. But first the reason had to be exhausted. Intuition functions only when reason is exhausted.

Intuition has no process; it simply jumps from the problem to the conclusion. It is a shortcut. It is a flash.

We have corrupted intuition. Man's intuition is almost absolutely corrupted. Woman's intuition is not corrupted as much— that's why women have something called a hunch. A hunch is just a fragment of intuition. It cannot be proved. You are going to take a flight somewhere, and the woman simply says that she is not going and she will not allow you to go either. She feels as if something is going to happen. Now this is nonsense—you have much work to do, everything is planned, and you have to go, but

> Woman's intuition is not corrupted as much—that's why women have something called a hunch. A hunch is just a fragment of intuition. It cannot be proved. Once your intuition has started functioning, you need not go and ask any outer guru for any advice.

the woman won't allow it. And the next day you read in the newspapers that the airplane was hijacked, or it crashed and all the passengers died. Now the woman cannot say how she knows. There is no way. It is just a hunch, just a feeling in the guts. But that too is corrupted, that's why it is just a flash.

When all the five other layers have disappeared and you have dropped fixed ideas—because you have been taught that reason is the only door to any conclusion—when you have dropped this fixation, this reason fixation, intuition starts flowering. Then it is not just like a flash, it is a constantly available source. You can close your eyes and you can go into it and always you can get the right direction from it. If those five layers are broken, then something arises in you that can be called an inner guide. You can always go into your intuition energy, and you will always find the right advice. In the East that is what they have called the inner guru, your inner master. Once your intuition has started functioning, you need not go and ask any outer guru for any advice.

Intuition is to be in tune with oneself, totally in tune with oneself. And out of that tuning, solutions arise from nowhere.

FUNCTION FROM THE FEMININE

The Zen master Goso Hoyen used to say:

When people ask me what Zen is like, I tell them this story:

Noticing that his father was growing old, the son of a burglar asked his father to teach him the trade so that he could carry on the family business after his father retired.

The father agreed, and that night they broke into a house together.

Opening a large chest, the father told his son to go in and pick out the clothing. As soon as the boy was inside, the father locked the chest and then made a lot of noise so that the whole house was aroused. Then he slipped quietly away.

Locked inside the chest, the boy was angry, terrified, and puzzled as to how he was going to get out. Then an idea flashed to him—he made a noise like a cat.

The family told a maid to take a candle and examine the chest.

When the lid was unlocked, the boy jumped out, blew out the candle, pushed his way past the astonished maid, and ran out. The people ran after him.

Noticing a well by the side of the road, the boy threw in a large stone, then hid in the darkness. The pursuers gathered around the well trying to see the burglar drowning himself.

When the boy got home, he was angry with his father and tried to tell him the story; but the father said,
"Don't bother to tell me the details. You are here—you
have learned the art."

Being is one, the world is many . . . and between the two is
the divided mind, the dual mind. It is just like a big tree, an ancient oak: the trunk is one, then the tree divides into two main
branches, the main bifurcation, from which a thousand and one
bifurcations of branches grow. The being is just like the trunk of
the tree—one, nondual—and the mind is the first bifurcation
where the tree divides into two, becomes dual, becomes dialect-
ical: thesis and antithesis, man and woman, yin and yang, day and
night, God and devil, Yoga and Zen. All the dualities of the
world are basically in the duality of the mind—and below the
duality is oneness of being. If you slip below, underneath the duality, you will find one—call it God, call it nirvana, or whatsoever you like.

If you go higher, through the duality, you come to the mil-
lionfold world.

This is one of the most basic insights to be understood—that
the mind is not one. Hence, whatsoever you see through the mind
becomes two. It is just like a white ray entering a prism; it is
immediately divided into seven colors and the rainbow is created.
Before it entered the prism it was one; through the prism it is
divided, and the white color disappears into the seven colors of
the rainbow.

The world is a rainbow, the mind is a prism, and the being is
the white ray.

Modern research has come to a significant fact, one of the most significant achieved in the twentieth century, and that is, you don't have one mind—you have two minds. Your brain is divided into two hemispheres, the right hemisphere and the left hemisphere. The right hemisphere is joined with the left hand, and the left hemisphere is joined with the right hand—crosswise. The right hemisphere is intuitive, illogical, irrational, poetic, platonic, imaginative, romantic, mythical, religious; and the left hemisphere is logical, rational, mathematical, Aristotelian, scientific, calculative.

These two hemispheres are constantly in conflict—the basic politics of the world is within you, the greatest politics of the world is within you. You may not be aware of it, but once you become aware, the real thing to be done is somewhere between these two minds.

The left hand is concerned with the right hemisphere—intuition, imagination, myth, poetry, religion—and the left hand is very much condemned. The society is of those who are right-handed—right-handed means the left hemisphere. Ten percent of children are born left-handed, but they are forced to be right-handed. Children who are born left-handed are basically irrational, intuitive, nonmathematical, noneuclidean—they are dangerous for society, so it forces them in every way to become right-handed. It is not just a question of hands, it is a question of inner politics: the left-handed child functions through the right hemisphere—which society cannot allow, it is dangerous, so he has to be stopped before things go too far.

It is suspected that in the beginning the proportion must have been fifty-fifty—left-handed children 50 percent and right-handed children 50 percent—but the right-handed party has ruled so long that by and by the proportion has fallen to 10 percent and 90 percent. Even amongst you here, many will be left-handed but you may not be aware of it. You may write with the right hand and do your work with the right hand, but in your childhood you may have been forced to be right-handed. This is a trick, because once you become right-handed, your left hemisphere starts functioning. The left hemisphere is reason; the right hemisphere is beyond reason, its functioning is not mathematical. It functions in flashes, it is intuitive—graceful, but irrational.

If you understand this division, you will understand many things. With the bourgeoisie and the proletariat, the proletariat is always functioning through the right hemisphere of the brain. The poor people are more intuitive. Go to the primitive people, they are more intuitive. The poorer the person, the less intellectual—and that may be the cause of his being poor. Because he is less intellectual, he cannot compete in the world of reason. He is less articulate as far as language is concerned, reason is concerned, calculation is concerned—he is almost a fool. That may be the cause of his being poor.

The rich person is functioning through the left hemisphere; he is more calculative, arithmetical in everything, cunning, clever, logical—and he plans. That may be the reason why he is rich.

The bourgeoisie and the proletariat cannot disappear by communist revolutions, no, because the communist revolution is by the same people. The czar ruled Russia; he ruled it through the left hemisphere of the mind. Then he was replaced by Lenin, who was of the same type. Then Lenin was replaced by Stalin, who was even more of the same type. The revolution is false because deep down the same type of people are ruling—the ruler and the ruled mean the same, and the ruled are those of the right-sided hemisphere. So whatsoever you do in the outside world makes no difference really, it is superficial.

The same applies to men and women. Women are right-hemisphere people, men are left-hemisphered. Men have ruled women for centuries. Now a few women are revolting, but the amazing thing is that these are the same type of women. In fact they are just like men—rational, argumentative, Aristotelian. It is possible that one day, just as the communist revolution succeeded in Russia and China, somewhere, maybe in America, women can succeed and overthrow men. But by the time the women succeed, the women will no longer be women, they will have become left-hemisphered. Because to fight, one has to be calculative, and to fight with men you have to be like men, aggressive. That very aggressiveness is shown all over the world in women's liberation. Women who have become part of that liberation movement are very aggressive, they are losing all grace, all that comes out of intuition. Because if you have to fight with men, you have to learn the same trick; if you have to fight with men, you have to fight with the same techniques.

Once you fight with somebody, by and by you have to use the same techniques and the same ways. Then the enemy may be defeated, but by the time he is defeated you have become your own enemy.

Fighting with anybody is dangerous because you become like your enemy. That is one of the greatest problems of humanity. Once you fight with somebody, by and by you have to use the same techniques and the same ways. Then the enemy may be defeated, but by the time he is defeated you have become your own enemy. Stalin is more czarlike than any czar, more violent than any czar. Of course it has to be so: to overthrow czars, very violent people are needed, more violent than the czar himself. Only they will become the revolutionaries, will come out on top. By the time they reach there, they have become czars themselves, and the society continues on the same path. Just superficial things change, deep down the same conflict remains.

> Stalin is more czarlike than any czar, more violent than any czar. Of course it has to be so: to overthrow czars, very violent people are needed, more violent than the czar himself.

The conflict is in man. Unless it is resolved there, it cannot be resolved anywhere else. The politics is within you; it is between the two parts of the mind.

A small bridge exists. If that bridge is broken through some accident, through some physiological defect or something else, the person becomes split, the person becomes two persons, and the phenomenon of schizophrenia or "split personality" happens. If the bridge is broken—and the bridge is fragile—then you become two, you behave like two persons. In the morning you are loving, beautiful; in the evening you are angry, absolutely different. You don't remember your morning—how can you remember? Another mind was functioning—and the person becomes two persons. If this bridge is strengthened so much that the two minds disappear as two and become one, then integration, then crystallization, arises. What George Gurdjieff used to call the "crystallization of being" is nothing but these two minds becoming one, the meeting of the male and the female within, the meeting of yin and yang, the meeting of left and right, the meeting of logic and illogic, the meeting of Plato and Aristotle.

If you can understand this basic bifurcation in your tree of the mind, then you can understand all the conflict that goes on around and inside you.

Let me tell you an anecdote:

Among the Germans, Berlin is considered the epitome of Prussian brusqueness and efficiency, while Vienna is the essence of Austrian charm and slipshoddery. There is the tale of a Berliner visiting Vienna who was lost and in need of directions. What would such a Berliner do? He grabbed at the lapel of the first passing Viennese and barked out, "The post office—where is it?"

The startled Viennese carefully detached the other's fist, smoothed his lapel, and said in a gentle manner, "Sir, would it not have been more delicate of you to have approached me politely and to have said, 'Sir, if you have a moment and happen to know, could you direct me to the post office?' "

The Berliner stared in astonishment for a moment,

then growled, "I would rather be lost!" and stomped away.

That very same Viennese was visiting Berlin that same year, and now he had to search for the post office. Approaching a Berliner, he said politely, "Sir, if you have a moment and happen to know, could you please direct me to the post office?"

With machinelike rapidity the Berliner replied, "About-face, two blocks forward, sharp turn right, one block forward, cross a street, half turn on the right, walk left over railroad tracks, pass newsstand into post office lobby."

The Viennese, more bewildered than enlightened, nevertheless murmured, "A thousand thanks, kind sir," whereupon the Berliner snatched furiously at the other's lapel and shouted, "Never mind the thanks—repeat the instructions!"

The male mind, the Berliner; the female mind, the Viennese. The female mind has grace, the male mind has efficiency. And of course in the long run, if there is a constant fight, the graceful is bound to be defeated and the efficient mind will win, because the world understands the language of mathematics, not of love. But the moment your efficiency wins over your grace, you have lost something tremendously valuable: you have lost contact with your own being. You may become very efficient, but you will no longer be a real person. You will become a machine, a robotlike thing.

Because of this there is constant conflict between men and women. They cannot remain separate, they have to get into relationship again and again, but they cannot remain together either. The fight is not outside, the fight is within you.

And this is my understanding: unless you have resolved your inner fight between the right and the left hemispheres, you will never be able to be peacefully in love—never—because the inner fight will be reflected outside. If you are fighting inside and you are identified with the left hemisphere, the hemisphere of reason, and you are continuously trying to overpower the right hemisphere, you will try to do the same with the woman you fall in love with. If the woman is continuously fighting her own reason inside, she will continuously fight the man she loves.

The female mind has grace, the male mind has efficiency. And of course in the long run, if there is a constant fight, the graceful is bound to be defeated and the efficient mind will win, because the world understands the language of mathematics, not of love.

All relationships—almost all, the exceptions are negligible, can be left out of account—are ugly. In the beginning they are beautiful—in the beginning you don't show the reality, in the beginning you pretend. Once the relationship settles and you relax, your inner conflict bubbles up and

> ❧
>
> Unless you have resolved your inner fight between the right and the left hemispheres of the brain, you will never be able to be peacefully in love—never—because the inner fight will be reflected outside.

starts being mirrored in your relationship. Then come fights, then come a thousand and one ways of nagging each other, destroying each other.

People come to me and they ask how to go deep in a relationship. I tell them, "First you go deep in meditation." Unless you are resolved within yourself, you will create more problems than you already have. If you move into relationship, all your problems will be multiplied. Just watch—the greatest and the most beautiful thing in the world is love, but can you find anything more ugly, more hell-creating?

Mulla Nasruddin once told me, "Well, I have been putting off the evil day for months, but I have got to go this time."

"Dentist or doctor?" I inquired.

"Neither," he said, "I am getting married."

People go on avoiding marriage, people go on putting it off. When someday they find it impossible to get out of it, only then they relax. If you are outside of it, it may look like a beautiful oasis in the desert—but as you come close, the oasis starts drying and disappearing. Once you are caught in it, it is an imprisonment—but remember, the imprisonment doesn't come from the other, it comes from within you.

If the left hemisphere of the brain goes on dominating you, you will live a successful life—so successful that by the time you are forty you will have ulcers; by the time you are forty-five, you will have had at least one or two heart attacks. By the time you are fifty you will be almost dead—but successfully dead! You may become a great scientist, but you will never become a great being. You may accumulate enough wealth, but you will lose all that is of worth. You may conquer the whole world like an Alexander, but your own inner territory will remain unconquered.

There are many attractions for following the left hemisphere. That is the worldly brain; it is more concerned with things—cars, money, houses, power, prestige. That is the orientation of the man whom in India we call a *grustha,* a householder.

> If the left hemisphere of the brain goes on dominating you, you will live a successful life—so successful that by the time you are forty you will have ulcers; by the time you are forty-five, you will have had at least one or two heart attacks.

The right hemisphere is the orientation of the sannyasin, one who is more interested in his own inner being, his inner peace, his blissfulness, and is less concerned about things. If they come easily, good; if they don't come, that is also good. He is more concerned with the moment, less concerned with the future; more concerned with the poetry of life, less concerned with the arithmetic of it.

I have heard an anecdote:

Finkelstein had made a huge killing at the races, and Muscovitz, quite understandably, was envious. "How did you do it, Finkelstein?" he demanded.

"Easy," said Finkelstein, "it was a dream."

"A dream?"

"Yes. I had figured out a three-horse parlay, but I was not sure about the third horse. Then the night before, I dreamed that an angel was standing over the head of my bed and kept saying, 'Blessings on you, Finkelstein, seven times seven blessings on you.' When I woke up, I realized that seven times seven is forty-eight, and that horse number seventy-eight was Heavenly Dream. I made Heavenly Dream the third horse in my parlay, and I just cleaned up, simply cleaned up."

Muscovitz said, "But, Finkelstein, seven times seven is forty-nine!"

Finkelstein said, "So you be the mathematician."

There is a way to follow life through arithmetic, and there is another way to follow life through dreams, through dreams and visions. They are totally different.

Just the other day somebody asked, "Are there ghosts, fairies, and things like that?" Yes, there are—if you move through the right hemisphere of the brain, there are. If you move through the left hemisphere, there are not. All children are right-hemisphered; they see ghosts and fairies all around. But you go on talking to them and putting them in their places and saying to them, "Nonsense. You are stupid. Where is the fairy? There is nothing, just a shadow." By and by you convince the child, the helpless child— by and by you convince him and he moves from the right-hemisphere orientation to the left hemisphere orientation. He has to—he has to live in your world. He has to forget his dreams, he has to forget all myth, he has to forget all poetry, he has to learn mathematics. Of course he becomes efficient in mathematics—and becomes almost crippled and paralyzed in life. Existence goes on getting farther and farther away, and he becomes just a commodity in the market, his whole life becomes just rubbish . . . although, of course, valuable in the eyes of the world.

A sannyasin is one who lives through the imagination, who lives through the dreaming quality of his mind. Who lives through poetry, who poeticizes about life, who looks through visions— then trees are greener than they look to you, then birds are more beautiful, then everything takes a luminous quality. Ordinary pebbles become diamonds; ordinary rocks are no longer ordinary— nothing is ordinary! If you look from the right hemisphere, everything becomes divine, sacred.

A man was sitting with his friend in a cafeteria drinking tea. He studied his cup and said with a sigh, "Ah, my friend, life is like a cup of tea."

The other considered that for a moment, then said, "But why? Why is life like a cup of tea?"

The first man replied, "How should I know? Am I a philosopher?"

The right hemisphere only makes statements about facts, it cannot give you reasons. If you ask, "Why?" it can only remain silent, there comes no response from it. If you are walking and you see a lotus flower and you say, "Beautiful!" and somebody says, "Why?"—what will you do? You will say, "How am I to know? Am I a philosopher?"

It is a simple statement, a very simple statement, in itself total, complete. There is no reason behind it and no result beyond it, it is a simple statement of fact. Read the Upanishads—they are simple statements of facts. They say, "God *is*—don't ask why." They will say, "Are we philosophers? How are we to know? God *is*." They say God is beautiful, they say God is near, closer than your heart, but don't ask why—they are not philosophers.

Look at the gospels and the statements of Jesus—they are simple. He says, "My God is in heaven. I am his son, he is my father." Don't ask why. He will not be able to prove it in a court, he will simply say, "I *know*." If you ask him by whom he has been told, by what authority he says these things, he will say, "It is by my own authority. I have no other authority."

That is the problem when a man like Jesus moves in the world. The rational mind cannot understand. He was not crucified for any other reason. He was crucified by the left hemisphere because he was a right-hemisphere man. He was crucified because of the inner conflict.

Lao Tzu says, "The whole world seems to be clever, only I

am muddleheaded; the whole world seems to be certain, only I am confused and hesitant." He is a right-hemisphered man.

The right hemisphere is the hemisphere of poetry and love. A great shift is needed; that shift is the inner transformation. Yoga is an effort to reach the oneness of being through the left hemisphere, using logic, mathematics, science, and trying to go beyond. Zen is just the opposite: the aim is the same, but Zen uses the right hemisphere to go beyond. Both can be used, but to follow Yoga is a very, very long path; it is almost an unnecessary struggle because you are trying to reach from reason to superreason, which is more difficult. Zen is easier because it is an effort to reach the superreason from irreason. Irreason is almost like superreason—there are no barriers. Yoga is like penetrating a wall and Zen is like opening a door. The door may not be closed at all, you just push it a little and it opens.

Now the story. It is one of the most beautiful among Zen anecdotes. Zen people talk through stories—they have to talk through stories because they cannot create theories and doctrines, they can only tell stories. They are great storytellers. Jesus goes on talking in parables, Buddha goes on talking in parables, Sufi mystics go on talking in parables—it is not coincidental. The story, the parable, the anecdote, is the way of the right hemisphere; logic, argument, proof, syllogism, is the way of the left hemisphere.

Listen to it:

Goso Hoyen used to say, "When people ask me what Zen is like, I tell them this story."

This story really tells what Zen is like—without defining, it indicates. A definition is not possible because Zen in its basic quality is indefinable. You can taste it, but you cannot define it; you can live it, but language is not sufficient to say it; you can show it, but you cannot say it. But through a story a little bit can be transferred. And this story really indicates, indicates perfectly, what Zen is like.

This is just a gesture, don't make it a definition, don't philosophize around it, let it be like lightning, a flash of understanding. It is not going to increase your knowledge, but it can give you a shift, a jerk, a change of gestalt. You can be thrown from one corner of the mind to another . . . and that is the whole point of the story.

Noticing that his father was growing old, the son of a burglar asked his father to teach him the trade so that he could carry on the family business after his father retired.

The trade of a burglar is not a scientific thing, it is an art. Burglars are as much born as poets; you cannot learn, learning won't help. If you learn, you will be caught because then the police will know more than you—they have accumulated centuries of learning.

A burglar is a born burglar. He lives through intuition, it is a knack. He lives through hunches—a burglar is feminine. He is not a businessman, he is a gambler; he risks all for almost nothing. His whole trade is of danger and risk. It is just like a religious man. Zen people say that religious people are also like burglars: in search of God they are also burglars. There is no way to reach God through logic or reason or accepted society, culture, civilization. They break the wall somewhere, they enter from the back door. If in the daylight it is not allowed, they enter in dark. If it is not possible to follow the crowd on the superhighway, they make their own individual paths in the forest. Yes, there is a certain similarity. You can reach God only if you are a burglar, an artist of how to steal the fire, how to steal the treasure.

The father was going to retire and the son asked, "Before you retire, teach me your trade."

The father agreed, and that night they broke into a house together.

Opening a large chest, the father told his son to go in and pick out the clothing. As soon as the boy was inside, the father locked the chest and then made a lot of noise so that the whole house was aroused. Then he slipped quietly away.

A real master the father must have been, no ordinary burglar.

Locked inside the chest, the boy was angry, terrified, and puzzled.

Of course, naturally! What type of teaching is this? He had been thrown in a dangerous situation. But that is the only way to teach something of the unknown. That is the only way to teach something of the right hemisphere.

The left hemisphere can be taught in schools: learning is possible, discipline is possible, gradual courses are possible. Then, by and by, moving from one class to another, you become a master of art and science and many things. But there cannot be any schools for the right hemisphere: it is intuitive, it is not gradual. It is sudden; it is like a flash, like lightning in the dark night. If it happens, it happens. If it doesn't happen, it doesn't happen; nothing can be done about it. You can only leave yourself in a certain situation where there is more possibility for it to happen.

That's why I say the old man must have been a real master.

Locked inside the chest, the boy was angry, terrified, and puzzled.

Now there was no logical way to get out of that chest: it was locked from the outside, the father had made a noise, the whole house was awake, people were moving around, searching, and the father had escaped. Now is there any logical way to get out of this chest? Logic simply fails, reason is of no use. What can you think? Mind suddenly stops—and that is what the father is doing, that is what it is all about. He is trying to force the son into a situation where the logical mind stops, because a burglar does not need a logical mind. If he follows a logical mind, he will be caught sooner or later by the police because they also follow the same logic.

It happened in the Second World War. For three years Adolf Hitler continued to win, and the reason was, he was illogical. All the other countries that were fighting with him were fighting logically. Of course, they had a great science of war, military training, and this and that, and they had experts who would say, "Now,

Hitler is going to attack from this side." And if Hitler had also been in his senses, he would have done that, because that was the weakest point in the enemy's defense. Of course the enemy has to be attacked where he is the weakest—it is logical. So they would be expecting Hitler at the weakest point, they would be gathering around the weakest point, and he would hit anywhere, unpredictably.

He would not even follow his own generals' advice; he had an astrologer who would suggest where to attack. Now this is something never done before—a war is not run by astrologers! Once Churchill understood, once the spies came with the report that they were not going to win with this man because he was absolutely illogical—that a foolish astrologer who didn't know anything about war, who had never been on the front, was deciding things, deciding by the stars . . . What have stars got to do with a war on the earth? Churchill immediately appointed a royal astrologer to the king and started following the royal astrologer. Then things started falling in line because now two fools were predicting things. Things became easier.

If a burglar is going to follow Aristotle, he will be caught sooner or later because the same Aristotelian logic is followed by the police. If you go through logic, then anybody who follows the logical method can catch you anywhere. A burglar has to be unpredictable; logic is not possible. He has to be illogical—so much so that nobody can predict him. But illogic is possible only if your whole energy moves through the right hemisphere.

Locked inside the chest, the boy was angry, terrified, and puzzled as to how he was going to get out.

How is a logical question. Hence he was terrified because there was no way—*how* was simply impotent.

Then an idea flashed to him—now, this is a shift. Only in dangerous situations where the left hemisphere cannot function does it, as a last resort, allow the right hemisphere to have its say. When it cannot function, when it feels that now there is nowhere to go, now it is defeated, then it says, why not give a chance to the oppressed, to the imprisoned part of the mind? Give that too a chance. Maybe . . . there can be no harm.

Then an idea flashed to him—he made a noise like a cat.

Now this is not logical. Making a noise like a cat? Simply an absurd idea. But it worked.

The family told a maid to take a candle and examine the chest.

When the lid was unlocked, the boy jumped out, blew out the candle, pushed his way past the astonished maid, and ran out. The people ran after him.

Noticing a well by the side of the road, the boy threw in a large stone, then hid in the darkness. The pursuers gathered around the well trying to see the burglar drowning himself.

This too is not of the logical mind. Because the logical mind needs time—the logical mind needs time to proceed, to think, to argue this way and that, all the alternatives. And there are a thousand and one alternatives. But when you are in such a situation, there is no time to think. If people are pursuing you, how can you think? Thinking is good when you are sitting in an armchair. With your eyes closed you can philosophize and think and argue, for this and against that, pro and con. But when people are pursuing you and your life is in danger, you have no time to think—one lives in the moment, one simply becomes spontaneous. It is not that the boy *decided* to throw the stone, it simply *happened*. It was not a conclusion, he was not thinking about doing it, he simply found himself doing it. He threw a stone in the well and hid himself in the darkness. And the pursuers stopped, thinking the burglar had drowned himself in the well.

> Thinking is good when you are sitting in an armchair. But when people are pursuing you and your life is in danger, you have no time to think—one lives in the moment, one simply becomes spontaneous.

When the boy got home, he was angry with his father and tried to tell him the story; but the father said, "Don't bother to tell me the details. You are here, you have learned the art."

What is the point of telling the details? They are useless.

Details are useless as far as intuition is concerned because intuition is never a repetition. Details are meaningful as far as logic is concerned; so logical people go into minute details, so that if the same situation happens again, they will be in control and they will know what to do. But in the life of a burglar the same situation never happens again.

And in real life also the same situation never happens again. If you have conclusions in your mind, you will become almost dead, you will not be responding. In life, response is needed, not reaction: you have to act out of nowhere, with no conclusions inside. With no center you have to act—you have to act into the unknown from the unknown.

And this is what Goso Hoyen used to say when people asked him what Zen is like. This story he would tell. Zen is exactly like burglary! It is an art, it is not a science. It is feminine, it is not male; it is not aggressive, it is receptive. It is not a well-planned methodology; it is spontaneity. It has nothing to do with theories, hypotheses, doctrines, scriptures; it has something to do with only one thing, and that is awareness.

What happened in that moment when the boy was inside the chest? In such a danger you cannot be sleepy, in such a danger your consciousness becomes sharp—has to. Life is at stake, you are totally awake.

That's how one should be totally awake each moment. And when you are totally awake, this shift happens. From the left hemisphere the energy moves to the right hemisphere.

Whenever you are alert, you become intuitive; flashes come to you, flashes from the unknown, out of the blue. You may not follow them—then you will miss much.

Whenever you are in such a corner that your logic fails, don't be desperate, don't become hopeless. Those moments may prove the greatest blessings in your life. Those are the moments that the left allows the right to have its way. Then the feminine part, the receptive part, gives you an idea. If you follow it, many doors will be opened. But it is possible you may miss it; you may say, "What nonsense!"

This boy could have missed. The idea was not normal, regular, logical—make a noise like a cat? For what? He could have asked, "Why?" and then he would have missed. But he could not ask because the situation was such—there was no other way. So he thought, "Let us try. What is the harm in it?" He used the clue.

> Whenever you are in such a corner that your logic fails, don't be desperate, don't become hopeless. Those moments may prove the greatest blessings in your life.

The father was right. He said, "Don't go into details, they are not important. You are back home, you have learned the art."

The whole art is how to function from the feminine part of the mind—because the feminine is joined with the whole, and the male is not joined with the whole. The male is aggressive, the male is constantly in struggle—the feminine is constantly in surrender, in deep trust. Hence the feminine body is so beautiful, so round. There is a deep trust and a deep harmony with nature. A woman lives in deep surrender—a man is constantly fighting, angry, doing this and that, trying to prove something, trying to reach somewhere.

Ask women if they would like to go to the moon. They will simply be amazed—for what? What is the point? Why take such trouble? The home is perfectly good. She is more interested in the immediate, here, now, and that gives her a harmony, a grace. Man is constantly trying to prove something. And if you want to prove, of course you have to fight and compete and accumulate.

> ∿
>
> Man has been forcing woman to be silent, not only outside, inside also—forcing the feminine part to keep quiet. Just watch within you. If the feminine part says something, you immediately jump upon it and say, "Illogical, absurd!"

Once a woman tried to get Dr. Johnson to talk with her, but he seemed to take little notice of her.

"Why, Doctor," she said archly, "I believe you prefer the company of men to that of women."

"Madam," replied Johnson, "I am very fond of the company of ladies. I like their beauty, I like their delicacy, I like their vivacity . . . and I like their silence."

Man has been forcing woman to be silent, not only outside, inside also—forcing the feminine part to keep quiet. Just watch within you. If the feminine part says something, you immediately jump upon it and say, "Illogical, absurd!" Dr. Johnson, trying to keep the woman silent.

The heart is feminine. You miss much in your life because the head goes on talking; it does not allow the heart. And the only quality in the head is that it is more articulate, cunning, dangerous, violent. Because of its violence it has become the leader inside, and that inside leadership has become an outside leadership for men. Men have dominated women in the outside world also; the grace is dominated by violence.

Mulla Nasruddin was invited to a school for a certain function. There was a rally of schoolchildren, and in the rally the procession had been arranged according to height—from the shortest up to the tallest. But the pattern was broken, the Mulla noticed, by the first boy heading the procession. He was a gangling youth who looked a head taller than the rest. "Why is he at the front?" asked Mulla. He asked a young girl, "Is he the leader of the school, the captain, or something like that?"

"No," she whispered, "he pinches."

The male mind goes on pinching, creating trouble—troublemakers become leaders. In the schools, all wise teachers choose the greatest troublemakers as captains of the classes and the schools—the troublemakers, the criminals. Once they are in a powerful post, their whole energy for troublemaking becomes helpful for the teacher. They start creating discipline—the same children!

Just watch the politicians in the world: when one party is in power, the opposite party goes on creating trouble in the country. They are the lawbreakers, the revolutionaries, and the party that is in power goes on creating the discipline. Once they are thrown out of power, *they* will create trouble. And once the opposite party comes into power, they become the guardians of discipline.

They are all troublemakers.

The male mind is a troublemaking phenomenon—hence it overpowers, it dominates. But deep down, although you may attain power, you miss life—and deep down, the feminine mind continues. Unless you fall back to the feminine and you surrender, unless your resistance and struggle become surrender, you will not know real life and the celebration of it.

I have heard one anecdote:

An American scientist once visited the offices of the great Nobel Prize–winning physicist Niels Bohr in Copenhagen and was amazed to find that over his desk was a horseshoe. It was securely nailed to the wall with the open end up in the approved manner, so it would catch the good luck and not let it spill out. The American said with a nervous laugh, "Surely you don't believe the horseshoe will bring you good luck, do you, Professor Bohr? After all, as a levelheaded scientist . . ."

Bohr chuckled, "I believe in no such thing, my good friend, not at all. I am scarcely likely to believe in such foolish nonsense. However, I am told that a horseshoe will bring you good luck whether you believe in it or not."

Look a little deeper, and just underneath your logic you will find fresh waters of intuition, fresh waters of trust, flowing.

Zen is the way of the spontaneous—the effortless effort, the way of intuition. A Zen master, Ikkyu, a great poet, has said, "I can see clouds a thousand miles away, hear ancient music in the pines."

This is what Zen is all about. You cannot see clouds a thousand miles away with the logical mind. The logical mind is like glass, too dirty, too covered with the dust of ideas, theories, doctrines. But you can see clouds a thousand miles away with the pure glass of intuition, with no thoughts—just pure awareness. The mirror is clean and the clarity supreme.

You cannot hear ancient music in the pines with the ordinary, logical mind. How can you hear the ancient music? Music once gone is gone forever.

But I tell you, Ikkyu is right. You can hear ancient music in the pines—I have heard it—but a shift, a total change, a change of gestalt, is needed. Then you can see Buddha preaching again and you can hear Buddha speaking again. You can hear the ancient music in the pines—because it is eternal music, it is never lost. You have lost the capacity to hear it. The music is eternal; once you regain your capacity, suddenly it is there again. It has always been there, only you were not there.

Be here now and you also can see clouds a thousand miles away and hear ancient music in the pines.

Change more and more toward the right hemisphere, become more and more feminine, more and more loving, surrendering, trusting, more and more close to the whole. Don't try to be an island—become part of the continent.

MOVE FROM THINKING TO FEELING

Intellect is a heavy thing, intelligence is more total. Intellect is borrowed, intelligence is your own. Intellect is logical, rational;

intelligence is more than logical. It is superlogical, it is intuitive. The intellectual person lives only through argument. Certainly, arguments can lead you up to a certain point, but beyond that, hunches are needed.

Even great scientists who work through reason come to a point where reason does not work, where they wait for a hunch, for some intuitive flash, for some light from the unknown. And it always happens: if you have worked hard with the intellect, and you don't think that intellect is all, and you are available to the beyond, someday a ray penetrates you. It is not yours; and yet it is yours because it is nobody else's. It comes from your innermost center. It looks as if it is coming from the beyond because you don't know where your center of intuition is.

The Sanskrit word *sadhumati* is beautiful. *Mati* means intelligence, and *sadhu* means sage: sagely intelligence. Not only intelligence, but sagely intelligence. There are people who may be rational but are not reasonable—to be reasonable is more than to be rational. Sometimes the reasonable person will be ready to accept the irrational too—because he is reasonable. He can understand that the irrational also exists. The rational person can never understand that the irrational also exists. He can only believe in the limited, logical syllogism.

> Sometimes the reasonable person will be ready to accept the irrational too—because he is reasonable. He can understand that the irrational also exists.

But there are things that cannot

be proved logically, and yet they are. Everybody knows they are, and nobody has ever been able to prove them. Love is—nobody has ever been able to prove what it is, or whether it is or not. But everybody knows—love is. Even people who deny—they are not ready to accept anything beyond logic—even they fall in love. When they fall in love, then they are in a difficulty, they feel guilty.

But love is.

And nobody is ever satisfied by intellect alone unless the heart is also fulfilled. These are the two polarities inside you: the head and the heart.

> *Intelligence is the inborn capacity to see, to perceive. Every child is born intelligent, then made stupid by the society. We educate him in stupidity, and sooner or later he graduates in stupidity.*

INTELLIGENCE IS THE INBORN CAPACITY TO SEE, to perceive. Every child is born intelligent, then made stupid by the society. We educate him in stupidity, and sooner or later he graduates in stupidity.

Intelligence is a natural phenomenon—just as breathing is, just as seeing is. Intelligence is the inner seeing; it is intuitive. It has nothing to do with intellect, remember. Never confuse intellect with intelligence, they are polar opposites. Intellect is of the head; it is taught by others, it is imposed on you. You have to cultivate it. It is borrowed, it is something foreign, it is not inborn.

But intelligence is inborn. It is your very being, your very

> ✎
>
> Intellect is of the head; it is taught by others, it is imposed on you. You have to cultivate it. It is borrowed, it is something foreign, it is not inborn. But intelligence is inborn. It is your very being, your very nature.

nature. All animals are intelligent. They are not intellectuals, true, but they are all intelligent. Trees are intelligent, the whole existence is intelligent, and each child is born intelligent. Have you ever come across a child who is stupid? It is impossible! But to come across a grown-up who is intelligent is rare; something goes wrong in between.

A friend has sent this beautiful story. I would like you to listen to it; it may help. The story is called "The Animal School."

The animals got together in the forest one day and decided to start a school. There was a rabbit, a bird, a squirrel, a fish, and an eel, and they formed a board of directors. The rabbit insisted that running be in the curriculum. The bird insisted that flying be in the curriculum. The fish insisted that swimming had to be in the curriculum, and the squirrel said that perpendicular tree climbing was absolutely necessary to the curriculum. They put all of these things together and wrote a curriculum guide. Then they insisted that all of the animals take all of the subjects.

Although the rabbit was getting an A in running, perpendicular tree climbing was a real problem for him.

He kept falling over backward. Pretty soon he got to be sort of brain-damaged and could not run anymore. He found that instead of making an A in running he was making a C, and of course he always made an F in perpendicular climbing. The bird was really beautiful at flying, but when it came to burrowing in the ground, he could not do so well. He kept breaking his beak and wings. Pretty soon he was making a C in flying as well as an F in burrowing, and he had a hell of a time with perpendicular tree climbing.

Finally, the animal who ended up being valedictorian of the class was a mentally retarded eel who did everything halfway. But the educators were all happy because everybody was taking all of the subjects, and it was called a "broad-based education."

We laugh at this, but that's how it is. It is what happened to you. We really are trying to make everybody the same as everybody else, hence destroying everybody's potential for being himself.

Intelligence dies in imitating others. If you want to remain intelligent, you will have to drop imitating. Intelligence commits suicide in copying, in becoming a carbon copy. The moment you start thinking how to be like that other person, you are falling from your intelligence, you are becoming stupid. The moment you compare yourself with somebody else, you are losing your natural potential. Now you will never be happy, and you will never be clean, clear, transparent. You will lose your clarity, you will lose your vision. You will have borrowed eyes; but how can you see through somebody else's eyes? You need your own eyes, you need your own legs to walk, your own heart to beat.

People are living a borrowed life, hence their life is paralyzed. This paralysis makes them look stupid.

A totally new kind of education is needed in the world. The person who is born to be a poet is proving himself stupid in mathematics, and the person who could have been a great mathematician is just cramming history and feeling lost. Everything is topsy-turvy because education is not according to your nature. It does not pay any respect to the individual, it forces everybody into a certain pattern. Maybe by accident the pattern fits a few people, but the majority are lost and the majority live in misery.

The greatest misery in life is to feel oneself stupid, unworthy, unintelligent—and nobody is born unintelligent; nobody can be born unintelligent because we come from existence. Existence is pure intelligence. We bring some flavor, some fragrance from the beyond, when we come into the world. But immediately the society jumps upon you, starts manipulating, teaching, changing, cutting, adding, and soon you have lost all shape, all form. The society wants you to be obedient, conformist, orthodox. This is how your intelligence is destroyed.

This is a prison cell in which you are living—you can drop it. It will be difficult to drop because you have become so accustomed to it. It will be difficult to drop because it is not just like clothing; it has become almost your skin, you have lived with it so long. It will be difficult to drop because this is your whole identity—but it has to be dropped if you really want to claim your real being.

If you really want to be intelligent, you have to be a rebel.

Only the rebellious person is intelligent. What do I mean by rebellion?—I mean dropping all that has been enforced on you
against your will. Search again for who you are, start from ABC
again. Think that your time, up to now, has been a wastage because you have been following.

No person is similar to anybody else, each is unique—that is
the nature of intelligence—and each is incomparable. Don't compare yourself to anybody. How can you compare? You are you
and the other is other. You are not similar, so comparison is not
possible.

But we have been taught to compare and we are continuously
comparing. Directly, indirectly, consciously, unconsciously, we live
in comparison. And if you compare, you will never respect yourself: somebody is more beautiful than you, somebody is taller than
you, somebody is healthier than you, and somebody is something
else; somebody has such a musical
voice . . . and you will be burdened
and burdened if you go on comparing. Millions of people are there;
you will be crushed by your com-
parisons.

And you had a beautiful soul, a
beautiful being that wanted to
bloom, that wanted to become a
golden flower, but you never allowed it.

Be unburdened. Put all aside.
Regain, reclaim your innocence,
your childhood. Jesus is right when

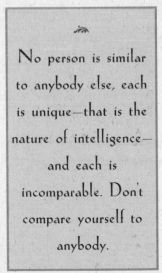

No person is similar
to anybody else, each
is unique—that is the
nature of intelligence—
and each is
incomparable. Don't
compare yourself to
anybody.

he says, "Unless you are born again, you shall not enter into my kingdom of God." I say the same to you: unless you are born again . . .

Drop all the garbage that has been put on you. Be fresh, start from the very beginning, and you will be surprised how much intelligence is immediately released.

Intelligence is the capacity to see, to understand, to live your own life according to your own nature. That is what intelligence is. And what is stupidity? Following others, imitating others, obeying others. Looking through their eyes, trying to imbibe their knowledge as your knowledge—that is stupidity.

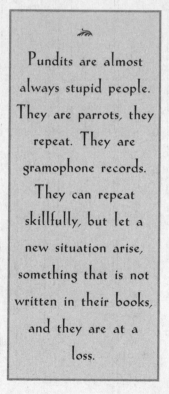

Pundits are almost always stupid people. They are parrots, they repeat. They are gramophone records.

They can repeat skillfully, but let a new situation arise, something that is not written in their books, and they are at a loss.

That's why pundits are almost always stupid people. They are parrots, they repeat. They are gramophone records. They can repeat skillfully, but let a new situation arise, something that is not written in their books, and they are at a loss. They don't have any intelligence. Intelligence is the capacity to respond moment to moment to life as it happens, not according to a program.

Only unintelligent people have a program. They are afraid; they know that they don't have enough intelligence to encounter life as it is. They have to be ready, they rehearse. They prepare the answer before the question has been raised—and that's how they prove themselves stupid, because the question is never the same. The question is always new. Each day brings its own problems, its own challenges, and each moment brings its own questions. And if you have ready-made answers in your head, you will not be able even to listen to the question. You will be so full of your answer, you will be incapable of listening. You will not be available. And whatsoever you will do, you will do according to your ready-made answer—which is irrelevant, which has no relationship with the reality as it is.

Intelligence is to relate with reality, unprepared. And the beauty of facing life unprepared is tremendous. Then life has a newness, a youth; then life has a flow and freshness. Then life has so many surprises. And when life has so many surprises, boredom never settles in you.

The stupid person is always bored. He is bored because of the answers that he has gathered from others and goes on repeating. He is bored because his eyes are so full of knowledge, he cannot see what is happening. He knows too much without knowing at all. He is not wise, he is only knowledgeable. When he looks at a rose, he does not look at *this* rose. All the roses that he has read about, all the roses that the poets have talked about, all the roses

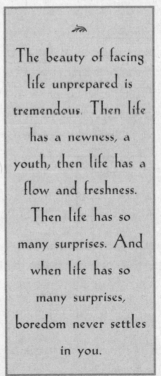

The beauty of facing life unprepared is tremendous. Then life has a newness, a youth, then life has a flow and freshness. Then life has so many surprises. And when life has so many surprises, boredom never settles in you.

that painters have painted and philosophers have discussed, and all the roses that he has heard about, they are standing in his eyes—a great queue of memories, information. This rose in front of him is lost in that queue, in that crowd. He cannot see it. He simply repeats; he says, "This rose is beautiful." Those words are also not his own, not authentic, not sincere, not true. Somebody else's voice . . . he is just playing a tape.

Stupidity is repetition, repeating others. It is cheap, cheap because you need not learn. Learning is arduous. One needs guts to learn. Learning means one has to be humble. Learning means one has to be ready to drop the old, one has to be constantly ready to accept the new. Learning means a nonegoistic state.

And one never knows where learning will lead you. One cannot predict about the learner; his life will remain unpredictable. He himself cannot predict what is going to happen tomorrow, where he will be tomorrow. He moves in a state of no-knowledge. Only when you live in no-knowledge, a constant state of no-knowledge, do you learn.

That's why children learn beautifully. As they grow old, they stop learning, because knowledge gathers and it is cheap to repeat it. Why bother? It is cheap, simple, to follow the pattern, to move in a circle. But then boredom settles. Stupidity and boredom go together.

The intelligent person is as fresh as dewdrops in the morning sun, as fresh as the stars in the night. You can feel his newness, so new, like a breeze.

Intelligence is the capacity to be reborn again and again. To die to the past is intelligence, and to live in the present is intelligence.

In fact, the intelligence of the head is not intelligence at all; it is knowledgeability. The intelligence of the heart *is* the intelligence, the only intelligence there is. The head is simply an accumulator. It is always old, it is never new, it is never original. It is good for certain purposes; for filing it is perfectly good. And in life one needs this—many things have to be remembered. The mind, the head, is a biocomputer. You can go on accumulating knowledge in it, and whenever you need, you can take it out. It is good for mathematics, good for calculation, good for the day-to-day life, the marketplace. But if you think this is your whole life, then you will remain stupid. You will never know the beauty of feeling, and you will never know the blessing of the heart. And you will never know the grace that descends only through the heart, the godliness that enters only through the heart. You will never know prayer, you will never know poetry, you will never know love.

The intelligence of the heart creates poetry in your life, gives dance to your steps, makes your life a joy, a celebration, a festivity, a laughter. It gives you a sense of humor. It makes you capable of love, of sharing. That is true life. The life that is lived from the head is a mechanical life. You become a robot—maybe very efficient; robots are efficient, machines are more efficient than man. You can earn much through the head, but you will not live much. You may have a better standard of living, but you won't have any life.

Life is of the heart. Life can only grow through the heart. It is in the soil of the heart where love grows, life grows, godliness grows. All that is beautiful, all that is really valuable, all that is meaningful, significant, comes through the heart. The heart is your very center, the head is just your periphery. To live in the head is to live on the circumference without ever becoming aware of the beauties and the treasures of the center. To live on the periphery is stupidity.

To live in the head is stupidity, and to live in the heart and use the head whenever needed is intelligence. But the center, the master, is at the very core of your being. The master is the heart and the head is just a servant—this is intelligence. When the head becomes the master and forgets all about the heart, that is stupidity.

It is up to you to choose. Remember, the head as a slave is a beautiful slave, of much utility, but as a master it is dangerous and will poison your whole life. Look around! People's lives are absolutely poisoned, poisoned by the head. They cannot feel, they are no longer sensitive, nothing thrills them. The sun rises but nothing rises in them; they look at the sunrise empty-eyed. The sky becomes full of the stars—the marvel, the mystery!—but nothing stirs in their hearts, no song arises. Birds sing, man has forgotten to sing. Clouds come in the sky and the peacocks dance, and man does not know how to dance. He has become a cripple. Trees bloom. Man thinks, never feels, and without feeling there is no flowering possible.

Watch, scrutinize, observe, have

> You owe it to yourself to have a deep, penetrating look at what you are doing with your life. Is there any poetry in your heart? If it is not there, then don't waste time. Help your heart to weave and spin poetry.

another look at your life. Nobody else is going to help you. You have depended on others so long; that's why you have become stupid. Now, take care; it is your own responsibility. You owe it to yourself to have a deep, penetrating look at what you are doing with your life. Is there any poetry in your heart? If it is not there, then don't waste time. Help your heart to weave and spin poetry. Is there any romance in your life? If not, then you are dead, then you are already in your grave.

Come out of it! Let life have something of the romantic in it, something like adventure. Explore! Millions of beauties and splendors are waiting for you. You go on moving around and around, never entering into the temple of life. The door is the heart.

Remember, this shift has to happen: from thinking you have to go to feeling. Feeling is closer, closer to something in you that is called intuition. Thinking is the farthest point from intuition. You have been taught by others—that is tuition. Something that has not been taught to you and blooms in you, that is intuition. Nobody has taught you, no school, no university, no college; nobody has said anything about it to you, it explodes in you—that is intuition. You need not go anywhere, you only need to go inside yourself.

Feeling is closer to intuition. I

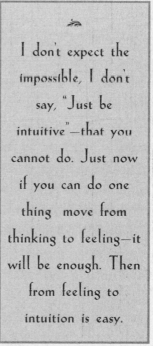

I don't expect the impossible, I don't say, "Just be intuitive"—that you cannot do. Just now if you can do one thing move from thinking to feeling—it will be enough. Then from feeling to intuition is easy.

don't expect the impossible, I don't say, "Just be intuitive"—that you cannot do. Just now if you can do one thing—move from thinking to feeling—it will be enough. Then from feeling to intuition is easy. But to move from thinking to intuition is difficult. They don't meet, they are polarities. Feeling is just in the middle. From feeling, thinking and intuition are at the same distance. If you go this way, you reach thinking; if you go that way, you reach intuition.

In feeling both meet and merge. Something of thinking remains in feeling, and something of intuition too.

RELAX

All that is great in science has come not through intellect but through intuition. All the great discoveries, all the great breakthroughs, have come from the beyond—from Archimedes to Albert Einstein.

You know the story of Archimedes—the discovery happened when he was lying in his tub enjoying a hot bath and suddenly, in that relaxed state . . . He had been very much worried for days—the king of the country had a beautiful golden crown, and he wanted to know whether it was made absolutely of gold, or if some other material was mixed in. And he wanted to know without the crown's being destroyed. Now this was a puzzle: How to determine the answer? How to know how much of the crown is gold and how much is some other metal? Archimedes tried hard; for nights he could not sleep, and there was no hope of finding the solution. But it happened.

The tub was full. When Archimedes went into the tub, some water went out of the tub—and like a flash, a lightning flash, the idea came to him: "The water going out of the tub must have something to do with my weight." And the thing clicked: "Now if we put gold into a full tub of water, some water will come out. That water will have something to do with the quantity of the gold."

And he was so thrilled. He was naked—he forgot all about nakedness, his ecstasy was so great. He rushed into the streets shouting, "Eureka! Eureka! I have found it! I have found it!"

It was an insight, not an intellectual conclusion.

Albert Einstein used to sit in the tub for hours—maybe just because of Archimedes! One of the great Indian intellectuals, Dr. Ram Manohar Lohia, went to see him—Dr. Lohia related the whole story to me. He was one of the most honest politicians India has known, and a keen observer of things, a great visionary, a genius. He was also educated in Germany, so he had many friends who knew Albert Einstein. Through some common friend the meeting was arranged. Dr. Lohia was exactly on time, but Albert Einstein's wife said, "You will have to wait, because he is in his bathtub and nobody knows when he will come out."

Half an hour passed, one hour passed, and Dr. Lohia asked the wife, "How long does it take?"

She said, "It is unpredictable."

Dr. Lohia asked, "What does he go on doing, sitting in the bathtub?"

The woman started laughing. "He plays with soap bubbles."

"For what?"

"It is when playing with soap bubbles that he has always arrived at certain insights for which he has been thinking and thinking but was failing and failing. It is always in his bathtub that insights flash into his mind."

Why in the bathtub? You are relaxed. And relaxation is the basis of meditation. You relax—when you relax, all tensions are dropped. Hot water, and the silence of the bathroom, and your aloneness . . . And now in the West, bathrooms are being made so beautiful they are almost like temples. A few people have even started making a sitting room in the bathroom! It is so beautiful— one can relax, one can meditate. In that meditative mood, things happen. The bathtub has always been a great provocateur. All the great scientists of the world are agreed upon it. Sometimes working for years for a certain conclusion and not arriving at it, and then one day suddenly it is there . . . out of nowhere, from the beyond.

> Whenever something comes from the mind, it is not science but only technology. Technology is a poor thing, it is not the insight but the implementation of the insight.

You cannot say it is a conclusion; it is not a conclusion at all.

Scientific discovery always arises out of meditation, not out of mind. And whenever something comes from the mind, it is not science but only technology. Technology is a poor thing; it is not the insight but the implementation of the insight. Technology comes out of the mind because mind itself is a technological device—a biological technology. All machines arise out of the mind, because mind itself is a machine. But no insight ever comes out of the mind, because no computer can ever give an insight. Insights come from the beyond. Mind is just the surface of your being; insights come from the center of your being. Meditation takes you to the center.

So when I say the mind is a wrong space, I mean don't get identified with the mind. Don't just become your mind—you are more, far more than the mind. Mind is only a small mechanism in you; use it, but don't get identified with it. Just as you drive your car—it is a mechanism, you use it, you don't become your car. The mind is a machine inside you, but don't become identified with it, there is no need. That identification creates a wrong space. When you start thinking "I am the mind," then you are in a wrong space. If you know "I am not the mind, but the master of the mind, I can use the mind," then mind is a good machine, of tremendous value. It can create great technology.

Science comes out of no-mind just as religiousness comes out of no-mind. Religion and science are not from separate sources, it is the same source—because both depend on breakthroughs, insights, intuitive flashes.

Technology comes out of the mind, and religious technology also comes out of the mind—yoga, man-

> When you start thinking "I am the mind," then you are in a wrong space. If you know "I am not the mind, but the master of the mind, I can use the mind," then mind is a good machine, of tremendous value.

tra, yantra. Yoga consists of body postures that can help you to go deep inside yourself—they are created by the mind. That is religious technology. That's why yoga is not part of any particular religion. There can be Christian yoga, there can be Hindu yoga, there is certainly Buddhist yoga, Jaina yoga—there can be as many yogas as there are religions. Yoga is just a technology. No machine is Hindu, no machine is Mohammedan. You don't go into the marketplace to purchase a Mohammedan car or a Hindu car. Machines are simply machines. Yoga is technology, mantra is technology, it is created by the mind. In fact the word *mantra* comes from the same root as *mind*—both come from the Sanskrit word *man*. One branch becomes "mind," another branch becomes "mantra"—both are part of the mind. Scientific technology is created by the mind, religious technology is created by the mind. All the rituals of religions—temples, mosques, churches, prayers, scriptures—these are all created by the mind.

But the flash, the insight, Buddha sitting under the bodhi tree . . . When for the first time he became aware, totally aware, that was not anything arising out of the mind. It was not part of the mind, it was something beyond. It was something that has nothing to do with you, with your ego, with your mind, with your body. It is something pure, virgin, it is part of the eternity. In that moment when Buddha's mind was completely at rest, the beyond penetrated him. He became a god.

Of course, for seven days he remained silent. The impact was such that he could not utter a single word. And the story says that the gods in heaven became disturbed, because it is rare that a man becomes a buddha, and if he remains silent, then who will teach the millions of people who are blind and groping in darkness? It is just a mythology, a beautiful story, but of significance and meaning. Those gods came, bowed down to Buddha, and prayed to him, "Speak! Tell people what you have attained."

And when Buddha started speaking, then it was coming out of the mind, then it was part of the mind. The phenomenon itself had happened in silence, but then he had to use words. Those words belong to the mind.

What I know is beyond mind, what I say to you is through mind. My words are part of the mind, but my knowing is not part of the mind.

FIND THE INNER GUIDE

You have a guide within you, but you don't use it. And you have not used it for so long, for so many lives, that you may not even be aware that a guide exists within you.

I was reading Castañeda's book. His master, Don Juan, gives him a beautiful experiment to do. It is one of the oldest experiments. On a dark night, on a hilly track, dangerous, without any light, Castañeda's master said, "You simply believe in the inner guide and start running." It was dangerous. It was a hilly track, unknown, with trees, bushes, abysses. Castañeda could fall anywhere. Even in the daylight he had to be alert walking there, and at night everything was dark. He could not see anything and his master said, "Don't walk, run!"

Castañeda couldn't believe it! It was simply suicidal. He became scared—but the master ran. He ran off just like a wild animal and came running back. And Castañeda could not understand how he was doing it. Not only was he running in this darkness, but each time he came running directly to Castañeda, as if he could see. Then by and by Castañeda gathered courage. If this old man could do this, why not he? He tried, and by and by he felt an inner light coming in. Then he started running.

You only *are* whenever you stop thinking. The moment you stop thinking, the inner happens. If you don't think, everything is okay—it is as if some inner guide is working. Your reason has misguided you. And the greatest misguidance has been this: you cannot believe in the inner guide.

First, you have to convince your reason. Even if your inner guide says, "Go ahead," you have to convince your reason, and then you miss opportunities. Because there are moments . . . you can use them or you can miss them. Intellect takes time, and while you are pondering, contemplating, thinking, you miss the moment. Life is not waiting for you. One has to live immediately. One has to be really a warrior, as they say in Zen, because when you are fighting in the field with your sword, you cannot think. You have to move without thinking.

Zen masters have used the sword as a technique for meditation, and they say in Japan that if two Zen masters, two meditative persons, are fighting with those swords, there can be no conclusion. No one can be

> *Intellect takes time, and while you are pondering, contemplating, thinking, you miss the moment. Life is not waiting for you. One has to live immediately.*

defeated and no one is going to win, because both are not thinking. The swords are just not in their hands, they are in the hands
of their inner guide, the nonthinking inner guide, and before the
other attacks, the guide knows and defends. You cannot think
about it because there is no time. The other is aiming at your
heart. In a flash of a moment the sword will penetrate to the heart.
There is no time to think about it, about what to do. When the
thought "penetrate the heart" occurs to him, simultaneously the
thought "defend" must occur to you—simultaneously, with no
gap—only then can you defend. Otherwise you will be no more.

So they teach swordsmanship as a meditation and they say,
"Be moment to moment with the inner guide, don't think. Allow
the inner being to do whatsoever happens to it. Don't interfere
with the mind." This is difficult because we are so trained with
our minds. Our schools, our colleges, our universities, the whole
culture, the whole pattern of civilization, teach our heads. We have
lost contact with the inner guide. Everyone is born with that inner
guide, but it is not allowed to work, to function. It is almost
paralyzed, but it can be revived.

Don't think with the head. Really, don't think at all. Just
move. Try it in some situations. It will be difficult, because the
old habit will be to start thinking. You will have to be alert—not
to think, but to feel inwardly what is coming to the mind. You
may be confused many times because you will not be able to know
whether it is coming from the inner guide or from the surface of
the mind. But soon you will know the feeling, the difference.

When something comes from the inner, it comes from your
navel upward. You can feel the flow, the warmth, coming from
the navel upward. Whenever your mind thinks, it is just on the

surface, in the head, and then it goes down. If your mind decided something, then you have to force it down. If your inner guide decides, then something bubbles up in you. It comes from the deep core of your being toward the mind. The mind receives it, but it is not of the mind. It comes from beyond—and that is why the mind is scared about it. For reason it is unreliable, because it comes from behind—without any reason with it, without any proofs. It simply bubbles up.

Try it in certain situations. For example, you have lost your path in a forest—try it. Don't think. Just close your eyes, sit down, be meditative, and don't think. Because it is futile—how can you think? You don't know. But thinking has become such a habit that you go on thinking even in moments when nothing can come out of it. Thinking can think only about something that is already known. You are lost in a forest, you don't have any map, there is nobody you can ask. What are you thinking about? But still you think. That thinking will be just a worry, not a thinking. And the more you get worried, the less the inner guide can be competent.

Be unworried. Sit down under a tree and just allow thoughts to drop and subside. Just wait, don't think. Don't create the prob-

> ⌘
>
> When something comes from the inner, it comes from your navel upward. You can feel the flow, the warmth, coming from the navel upward. Whenever your mind thinks, it is just on the surface, in the head.

lem, just wait. And when you feel a moment of nonthinking has come, then stand up and start moving. Wheresoever your body moves, allow it to move. You just be a witness. Don't interfere. The lost path can easily be found. But the only condition is, don't allow the mind to interfere.

This has happened many times unknowingly. Great scientists say that whenever a great discovery has been made, it was never made by the mind; it was always made by the inner guide.

When your mind gets exhausted and cannot do any more, it simply retires. In that moment of retirement the inner guide can give hints, clues, keys. The man who won the Nobel Prize for the inner structure of a human cell saw it in a dream. He saw the whole structure of the human cell, the inner cell, in a dream, and then in the morning he just made a picture of it. He himself couldn't believe that it could be so, so he had to work for years. After years of work he could conclude that the dream was true.

With Madame Curie it happened that when she came to know this process of the inner guide, she decided to try it. When once she had a problem to solve, she thought, "Why worry about it, and why try? Just go to sleep." She slept well, but there was no solution. So she was puzzled. Many times she tried: when there was a problem, immediately she would go to sleep—but there was no solution.

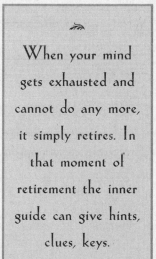

When your mind gets exhausted and cannot do any more, it simply retires. In that moment of retirement the inner guide can give hints, clues, keys.

First, the intellect has to be tried completely; only then can the solution bubble up. The head has to be completely exhausted; otherwise it goes on functioning, even in a dream.

So now scientists say that all the great discoveries are intuitive, not intellectual. This is what is meant by the inner guide.

Lose the head and drop into this inner guide. It is there. Old scriptures say that the master or the guru—the "outer" guru—can be helpful only in finding the inner guru. That is all. Once the outer guru has helped you to find the inner guru, the function of the outer guru is no more.

You cannot reach to the truth through a master; you can reach only to the inner master through a master—and then this inner master will lead you to the truth. The outer master is just a representative, a substitute. He has his inner guide and he can feel your inner guide also, because they both exist on the same wavelength—they both exist in the same tuning and the same dimension. If I have found my inner guide, I can look into you and feel your inner guide. And if I am really a guide to you, all my guidance will be to lead you to your inner guide. Once you are in contact with the inner guide, I am no longer needed. Now you can move alone.

So all that a guru can do is to push you down from your head to your navel, from your reasoning to your intuitive force, from your argumentative mind to your trusting guide. And it is not like this only with human beings, it is so with animals, with birds, with trees, with everything. The inner guide exists, and many new phenomena have been discovered that are mysteries.

There are a number of cases. For example, the mother fish dies immediately after she lays the egg. Then the father helps the

egg to be fertilized, and then he dies. The egg remains alone without a mother and without a father. It matures. Then a new fish is
born. This fish doesn't know anything about father, mother, parents; she doesn't know from where they came. But although this
particular fish lives in a particular part of the sea, she will move
to the part from where the father and the mother came to lay her
eggs. She will move to the source. This has been happening again
and again, and when she wants to lay an egg, she will come to
this bank, lay the egg, and die. So there is no communication
between parents and their children, but the children somehow
know where they have to go, where they have to move—and
they never miss. And you cannot misguide them. It has been tried,
but you cannot misguide them. They will reach to the source.
Some inner guide is working.

In Soviet Russia they were experimenting with cats, with rats,
and with many small animals. A cat, a mother cat, was separated
from her children, and the children were taken deep down into
the sea; the mother could not know what was happening to her
children. Every type of scientific instrument was attached to the
cat to measure what was going on within her mind and her heart,
and then one child was killed, deep in the sea. Immediately the
mother became aware. Her heart rate changed. She became puzzled and worried, her heartbeat increased as soon as the child was
killed. And the scientific instrument said that she was feeling severe
pain. Then after a while everything became normal. Then another
child was killed—again the change. And the same with the third
child. It happened every time, exactly at the same time, without
any time gap. What was happening?

The scientists say the mother has an inner guide, an inner

feeling center, and it is joined to her children, wherever they are. And she immediately feels a telepathic relationship. The human mother will not feel so much. This is puzzling—it should be quite otherwise: the human mother should feel more because she is more evolved. But she will not, because the head has taken everything into its hands and the inner centers are all lying paralyzed.

Whenever you are puzzled in a situation and you cannot see how to get out of it, don't think; just be in a deep nonthinking and allow the inner guide to guide you. In the beginning you will feel afraid, insecure. But soon, when you come every time to the right conclusion, when you come every time to the right door, you will gather courage and you will become trusting.

Wisdom comes from the heart, it is not of the intellect. Wisdom comes from the innermost depth of your being, it is not of the head.

Cut your head off, be headless—and follow the being wherever it leads. Even if it leads into danger, go into danger, because that will be the path for you and your growth. Follow it, trust it, and move with it.

MAKE HAPPINESS THE CRITERION

Does a person living through intuition always succeed? No, but he is always happy, whether he succeeds or not. And a person not living intuitively is always unhappy, whether he succeeds or not. Success is not the criterion, because success depends on many things. Happiness is the criterion because happiness depends only on you. You may not succeed because others are competitors.

Even if you are working intuitively, others may be working more cunningly, more cleverly, more calculatingly, more violently, more immorally. So success depends on many other things; success is a social phenomenon. You may not succeed.

Who can say that Jesus succeeded? Crucifixion is not a success, it is the greatest failure. A man crucified when he was just thirty-three—what type of success is this? No one knew about him. Just a few villagers, uneducated people, were his disciples. He had no position, no prestige, no power. What type of success is this? Crucifixion cannot be said to be a success. But he was happy. He was totally blissful—even when being crucified. And those who were crucifying him would remain alive for many years, but they would remain in misery. So really, who was undergoing crucifixion? That is the point. Those who crucified Jesus, were they undergoing crucifixion, or was Jesus, who was crucified? He was happy—how can you crucify happiness? He was ecstatic—how can you crucify ecstasy? You can kill the body but you cannot kill the soul. Those who crucified him, they lived, but their life was nothing but a long, slow crucifixion—misery and misery and misery.

So the first thing is that I don't say that if you follow the inner guide of your intuition, you will always succeed in the sense that the world recognizes success. But in the sense that a Buddha or a Jesus recognizes success, you will succeed. And that success is measured by your happiness, your bliss—whatsoever happens is irrelevant, you will be happy. Whether the world says that you have been a failure or the world makes you a star, a success, it doesn't make any difference. You will be happy whatever the case; you will be blissful. Bliss is success to me. If you can understand that bliss is success, then I say you will succeed always.

But to you bliss is not success; success is something else. It may even be misery. Even if you know that it is going to be a misery, you long for success. We are ready to be miserable if success comes to us. So what is success to us? Success is ego fulfillment, not bliss. It is just so that people will say that you have succeeded. You may have lost everything—you may have lost your soul; you may have lost all that innocence that gives bliss; you may have lost all that peace, silence, that brings you nearer to the divine. You may have lost all and become just a madman—but the world will say you are a success.

For the world, ego gratification is the success; for me it is not. For me, to be blissful is success—whether anyone knows about you or not. It is irrelevant whether anyone knows about you or not, whether you live totally un-known, unheard of, unnoticed. But if you are blissful, you have suc-ceeded.

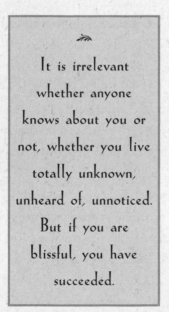

It is irrelevant whether anyone knows about you or not, whether you live totally unknown, unheard of, unnoticed. But if you are blissful, you have succeeded.

So remember this distinction because many people would like to be intuitive, would like to find the inner guide, just to succeed in the world. For them the inner guide will be a frustration. In the first place they cannot find it. In the second place, even if they can find it, they will be miserable. Because what they are aiming at is recognition by the world, ego fulfillment—not bliss.

Be clear in the mind—don't be success-oriented. Success is the greatest failure in the world. So don't try to succeed, otherwise you will be a failure. Think of being blissful. Every moment think of being more and more blissful. Then the whole world may say you are a failure, but you will not be a failure. You have attained.

Buddha was a failure in the eyes of his friends, family, wife, father, teachers, society—he was a failure. He had become just a beggar. What

> Many people would like to be intuitive, would like to find the inner guide, just to succeed in the world. For them the inner guide will be a frustration.

type of success is this? He could have been a great emperor; he had the qualities, he had the personality, he had the mind. He could have been a great emperor, but he became a beggar. He was a failure—obviously. But I say to you he was not a failure. If he had become an emperor, then he would have been a failure because he would have missed his real life. What he attained under the bodhi tree was the real, and what he lost was unreal.

With the real you will succeed in the inner life; with the unreal . . . I don't know. If you want to succeed in the unreal, then follow the path of those who are working with cunningness, cleverness, competition, jealousy, violence. Follow their path, the inner guide is not for you. If you want to gain something of the world, then don't listen to the inner guide.

But ultimately you will feel that although you have won the

whole world, you have lost yourself. Jesus says, "And what does a man get if he loses his soul and gains the whole world?" Whom will you call a success—Alexander the Great or Jesus the crucified?

So if—and that *if* has to be understood well—if you are interested in the world, then the inner guide is not a guide for you. If you are interested in the inner dimension of being, then the inner guide, and only the inner guide, can help.

GO FOR THE POETRY

Many things cannot be expressed in Western languages, because the Eastern approach toward reality is basically, fundamentally, tacitly different. Sometimes it happens, the same thing can be looked at in the Eastern and in the Western way, and on the surface the conclusions may look similar, but they cannot be. If you go a little deeper, if you dig a little deeper, you will find great differences— not ordinary differences but extraordinary differences.

Just the other night I was reading the famous haiku of Bashō, the Zen mystic and master. It does not look like great poetry to the Western mind, or to the mind that has been educated in a Western way. And now the whole world is being educated in the Western way; East and West have disappeared as far as education is concerned.

Listen to it silently, because it is not what you call great poetry, but it is great insight—which is far more important. It has tremendous poetry, but to feel that poetry you have to be subtle. Intellectually, it cannot be understood; it can be understood only intuitively.

This is the haiku:

When I look carefully,
I see the nazunia blooming
by the hedge!

Now, there seems to be nothing of great poetry in it. But let us go into it with more sympathy, because Bashō is being translated into English; in his own language it has a totally different texture and flavor.

The nazunia is a common flower—grows by itself by the side of the road, a grass flower. It is so common that nobody ever looks at it. It is not a precious rose, it is not a rare lotus. It is easy to see the beauty of a rare lotus floating on a lake—a blue lotus, how can you avoid seeing it? For a moment you are bound to be caught by its beauty. Or a beautiful rose dancing in the wind, in the sun . . . for a split second it possesses you. It is stunning. But a nazunia is an ordinary, common flower. It needs no gardening, no gardener; it grows by itself anywhere. To see a nazunia carefully a meditator is needed, a delicate consciousness is needed; otherwise you will pass it by. It has no apparent beauty, its beauty is deep. Its beauty is that of the ordinary, but the ordinary contains the extraordinary in it—even the nazunia. Unless you penetrate it with a sympathetic heart, you will miss it.

When for the first time you read Bashō, you start thinking, "What is there so tremendously important to say about a nazunia blooming by the hedge?"

In Bashō's poem the last syllable—*kana* in Japanese—is translated by an exclamation point because we don't have any other way to translate it. But *kana* means "I am amazed!" Now, from where is the beauty coming? Is it coming from the nazunia?—because thousands of people may have passed by the side of the hedge and nobody may even have looked at this small flower. And Bashō is possessed by its beauty, is transported into another world. What has happened?

It is not really the nazunia, otherwise it would have caught everybody's eye. It is Bashō's insight, his open heart, his sympathetic vision, his meditativeness. Meditation is alchemy: it can transform the base metal into gold, it can transform a nazunia flower into a lotus.

When I look carefully . . .

And the word *carefully* means attentively, with awareness, mindfully, meditatively, with love, with caring. One can just look without caring at all, and then one will miss the whole point. That word *carefully* has to be remembered in all its meanings, but the root meaning is "meditatively." And what does it mean when you see something meditatively? It means without mind, looking without the mind, no clouds of thought in the sky of your consciousness, no memories passing by, no desires . . . nothing at all, utter emptiness.

When in such a state of no-mind you look, even a nazunia is transported into another world. It becomes a lotus of paradise, it is no longer part of the earth; the extraordinary has been found in the ordinary. And this is the way of a buddha. To find the extraordinary in the ordinary, to find all in the now, to find the whole in this—Gautam Buddha calls it *tathata*.

Bashō's haiku is a haiku of *tathata*. This nazunia—looked at lovingly, caringly through the heart, unclouded consciousness, in a state of no-mind—and one is amazed, one is in awe. A great wonder arises: How is it possible? This nazunia—and if a nazunia is possible, then everything is possible. If a nazunia can be so beautiful, Bashō can be a buddha. If a nazunia can contain such poetry, then each stone can become a sermon.

When I look carefully, I see the nazunia blooming by the hedge!

Kana—I am amazed! I am struck dumb; I cannot say anything about its beauty—I can only hint at it.

A haiku simply hints, the haiku only indicates—and in an indirect way.

A similar situation is found in Tennyson's famous poetry; comparing both will be of great help to you. Bashō represents the intuitive, Tennyson the intellectual. Bashō represents the East, Tennyson the West. Bashō represents meditation, Tennyson mind. They look similar, and sometimes the poetry of Tennyson may look more poetic than Bashō's because it is direct, it is obvious.

> *Flower in the crannied wall,*
> *I pluck you out of the crannies,*
> *I hold you here, root and all, in my hand,*
> *Little flower—but if I could understand*
> *What you are, root and all, and all in all,*
> *I should know what God and man is.*

A beautiful piece, but nothing compared to Bashō. Let us see where Tennyson becomes totally different.

First: *Flower in the crannied wall, I pluck you out of the crannies . . .*
Bashō simply looks at the flower, he does not pluck it out.

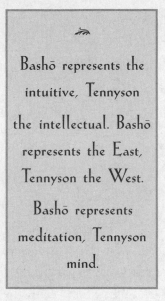

Bashō represents the intuitive, Tennyson the intellectual. Bashō represents the East, Tennyson the West. Bashō represents meditation, Tennyson mind.

Bashō is a passive awareness, Tennyson is active, violent. In fact, if you have really been impressed by the flower, you cannot pluck it. If the flower has reached your heart, how can you pluck it? Plucking it means destroying it, killing it—it is murder! Nobody has thought about Tennyson's poetry as murder—but it is murder. How can you destroy something so beautiful?

But that's how our mind functions; it is destructive. It wants to possess, and possession is possible only through destruction.

Remember, whenever you possess something or somebody, you destroy something or somebody. You possess the woman?—you destroy her, her beauty, her soul. You possess the man?—he is no longer a human being; you have reduced him to an object, into a commodity.

Bashō looks "carefully"—just looks, not even gazes concentratedly. Just a look, soft, feminine, as if afraid to hurt the nazunia.

Tennyson plucks it out of the crannies and says:

I hold you here, root and all, in my hand, little flower . . .

He remains separate. The observer and the observed are nowhere melting, merging, meeting. It is not a love affair. Tennyson attacks the flower, plucks it out root and all, holds it in his hand.

Mind always feels good whenever it can possess, control, hold. A meditative state of consciousness is not interested in possessing, in holding, because all those are the ways of the violent mind.

And Tennyson says *"little flower"*—the flower remains little, he remains on a high pedestal. He is a man, a great intellectual, a great poet. He remains in his ego: "little flower."

For Bashō, there is no question of comparison. He says nothing about himself, as if he is not. There is no observer. The beauty is such that it brings a transcendence. The nazunia flower is there, blooming by the hedge—*kana*—and Bashō is simply amazed, is struck to the very roots of his being. The beauty is overpowering. Rather than possessing the flower, he is possessed by the flower. He is in a total surrender to the beauty of the flower, to the beauty of the moment, to the benediction of the herenow.

> Mind always feels good whenever it can possess, control, hold. A meditative state of consciousness is not interested in possessing, in holding, because all those are the ways of the violent mind.

Little flower, says Tennyson, *but if I could understand . . .*

That obsession to understand! Appreciation is not enough, love is not enough; understanding has to be there, knowledge has to be produced. Unless knowledge is arrived at, Tennyson cannot be at ease. The flower has become a question mark. For Tennyson it is a question mark, for Bashō it is an exclamation point.

And there is the great difference: the question mark and the exclamation point.

Love is enough for Bashō. Love *is* understanding. What more understanding can there be? But Tennyson seems to know nothing of love. His mind is there, hankering to know.

But if I could understand what you are, root and all, and all in all . . .

And mind is compulsively perfectionist. Nothing can be left unknown, nothing can be allowed to remain unknown and mysterious. *Root and all, and all in all*, has to be understood. Unless mind knows everything, it remains afraid—because knowledge gives power. If there is something mysterious, you are bound to remain afraid because the mysterious cannot be controlled. And who knows what is hidden in the mysterious? Maybe the enemy, maybe a danger, some insecurity? And who knows what it is going to do to you? Before it can do anything, it has to be understood, it has to be known. Nothing can be left as mysterious.

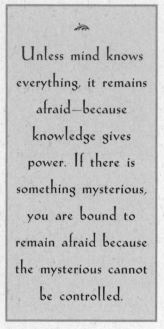

Unless mind knows everything, it remains afraid—because knowledge gives power. If there is something mysterious, you are bound to remain afraid because the mysterious cannot be controlled.

But then all poetry disappears, all love disappears, all mystery disappears, all wonder disappears. The soul disappears, the song disappears, the celebration disappears. All is known—then nothing is valuable. All is known—then nothing is of any worth. All is known—then there is no meaning in life, no significance in life.

See the paradox: first the mind says, "Know everything!"—

and when you have known it, the mind says, "There is no meaning in life."

You have destroyed the meaning, and now you are hankering for meaning. The mind is destructive of meaning. And because it insists everything can be known, it cannot allow the third category, the unknowable—which will remain unknowable eternally. And in the unknowable is the significance of life.

All the great values—of beauty, of love, of God, of prayer— all that is really significant, all that makes life worth living, is part of the third category: the unknowable. The unknowable is another name for God, another name for the mysterious and the miraculous. Without it there can be no wonder in your heart—and without wonder, a heart is not a heart at all, and without awe you lose something tremendously precious. Then your eyes are full of dust, they lose clarity. Then the bird goes on singing but you are unaffected, unstirred, your heart is not moved—because you know the explanation.

The trees are green, but the greenness does not transform you into a dancer, into a singer. It does not trigger a poetry in your being, because you know the explanation: it is chlorophyll that is making the trees green. So nothing of poetry is left. When the explanation is there, the poetry disappears. And all explanations are utilitarian, they are not ultimate.

If you don't trust the unknowable, then how can you say that the rose is beautiful? Where is the beauty? It is not a chemical component of the rose. The rose can be analyzed and you will not find any beauty in it. If you don't believe in the unknowable, you can do an autopsy on a man, a postmortem—you will not find any soul. And you can go on searching for God and you will not find him anywhere, because he is everywhere. The mind is going to miss him, because the mind would like him to be an object and God is not an object.

God is a vibe. If you are attuned to the soundless sound of existence, if you are attuned to one hand clapping, if you are attuned to what the Indian mystics have called *anahat*—the ultimate music of existence—if you are attuned to the mysterious, you will know that *only* God is, and nothing else. Then God becomes synonymous with existence.

But these things cannot be understood, these things cannot be reduced to knowledge—and that's where Tennyson misses, misses the whole point. He says:

Little flower—but if I could understand what you are, root and all, and all in all, I should know what God and man is.

But it is all "but" and "if."

Bashō *knows* what God is and what man is in that exclamation mark—*kana*. "I am amazed, I am surprised . . . *nazunia blooming by the hedge!*"

Maybe it is a full-moon night, or maybe it is early morning—I can actually see Bashō standing by the side of the road, not moving, as if his breath has stopped. A nazunia . . . and so beautiful. All past is gone, all future has disappeared. There are no more questions in his mind, just sheer amazement. Bashō has become a child. Again those innocent eyes of a child looking at a nazunia, carefully, lovingly. And in that love, in that care, is a totally different kind of understanding—not intellectual, not analytical. Tennyson intellectualizes the whole phenomenon and destroys its beauty.

Tennyson represents the West, Bashō represents the East. Tennyson represents the male mind, Bashō represents the feminine mind. Tennyson represents the mind, Bashō represents the no-mind.

Afterword

❧

NO DESTINATION

The distinction is subtle, but it is the same distinction as between the mind and the heart, between logic and love, or even more appropriate, between prose and poetry.

A destination is a clear-cut thing; direction is intuitive. A destination is something outside you, more like a thing. A direction is an inner feeling; not an object, but your very subjectivity. You can feel direction, you cannot know it. You can know the destination, you cannot feel it. Destination is in the future. Once decided, you start manipulating your life toward it, steering your life toward it.

How can you decide the future? Who are you to decide the unknown? How is it possible to fix the future? Future is that which is not known yet. Future is open possibility. By your fixing a destination your future is no longer a future, because it is no longer open. Now you have

> ❧
>
> By your fixing a destination your future is no longer a future, because it is no longer open. Now you have chosen one alternative out of many.

187

chosen one alternative out of many, because when all the alternatives were open, it was future. Now all alternatives have been dropped; only one alternative has been chosen. It is no longer future, it is your past.

When you decide a destination, it is the past that decides. Your experience of the past, your knowledge of the past decides. You kill the future—then you go on repeating your past, maybe a little modified, a little changed here and there according to your comfort, convenience. Repainted, renovated, but still it comes out of the past. This is the way one loses track of the future: by deciding a destination, one loses track of the future. One becomes dead, one starts functioning like a mechanism.

Direction is something alive, in the moment. It knows nothing of the future, it knows nothing of the past, but it throbs, pulsates, here and now. And out of this pulsating moment, the next moment is created. Not by any decision on your part—but just because you live this moment and you live it so totally, and you love this moment so wholly, out of this wholeness the next moment is born. It is going to have a direction. That direction is not given by you, it is not imposed by you; it is spontaneous.

You cannot decide direction, you can only live this moment that is available to you. By living it, di-

> You go on repeating your past, maybe a little modified, a little changed here and there according to your comfort, convenience. Repainted, renovated, but still it comes out of the past.

rection arises. If you dance, the next moment is going to be of a deeper dance. Not that you decide, but you simply dance this moment. You have created a direction, you are not manipulating it. The next moment will be more full of dancing, and still more will be following.

Destination is fixed by the mind; direction is earned by living. Destination is logical: one wants to be a doctor, one wants to be an engineer, one wants to be a scientist, or one wants to be a politician. One wants to be a rich man, famous man—these are destinations. Direction?—one simply lives the moment in deep trust that life will decide. One lives this moment so totally that out of this totality a freshness is born. Out of this totality the past dissolves and the future starts taking shape. But this shape is not given by you, this shape is earned by you.

> You cannot decide direction, you can only live this moment that is available to you. By living it, direction arises. If you dance, the next moment is going to be of a deeper dance.

One Zen master, Rinzai, was dying; he was on the deathbed. Somebody asked, "Master, people will ask after you are gone, what was your essential teaching? You have said many things, you have talked about many things—it will be difficult for us to condense it. Before you leave, please, you yourself condense it into a single sentence, so we will treasure it. And whenever people who have not known you desire, we can give them your essential teaching."

Dying, Rinzai opened his eyes, gave a great Zen shout, a lion's roar! They were all shocked! They couldn't believe that this dying man could have so much energy. They were not expecting it. The man was unpredictable, he had always been so, but even with this unpredictable man they were not in any way expecting that dying, at the last moment, he would give such a lion's roar. And when they were shocked—and of course their minds stopped, they were surprised, taken aback—Rinzai said, "This is it!" closed his eyes, and died.

This is it. . . .

This moment, this silent moment, this moment uncorrupted by thought, this silence that was surrounding this surprise, this last lion's roar over death—this is it.

Yes, direction comes out of living this moment. It is not something that you manage and plan. It happens, it is subtle, and you will never be certain about it. You can only feel it. That's why I say it is more like poetry, not like prose; more like love, not like logic; more like art than like science. And that's its beauty—hesitant, as hesitant as a dewdrop on a grass leaf, slipping, not knowing where, not knowing why. In the morning sun, just slipping on a leaf of grass.

Direction is subtle, delicate, fragile.

Destination belongs to the ego; direction belongs to life, to being.

To move in the world of direction one needs tremendous trust, because one is moving in insecurity, one is moving in darkness. But the darkness has a thrill in it: without any map, without any guide, you are moving into the unknown. Each step is a discovery, and it is not only a discovery of the outside world. Simultaneously, something is discovered in you also. A discoverer not only discovers things. As he goes on discovering more and more unknown worlds, he goes on discovering himself also, simultaneously. Each discovery is an inner discovery also. The more you know, the more you know about the knower. The more you love, the more you know about the lover.

I am not going to give you a destination. I can only give you a direction—awake, throbbing with life and unknown, always surprising, unpredictable. I'm not going to give you a map. I can give you only a great passion to discover.

Yes, a map is not needed; great passion, great desire to discover, is needed. Then I leave you alone. Then you go on your own. Move into the vast, into the infinite, and by and by, learn to trust it. Leave yourself in the hands of life. The man who trusts, the man who is thrilled even at the gate of death—he can give a lion's roar. Even dying—because he knows nothing dies—at the very moment of death he can say, "This is it!"

Because each moment, this is it. It may be life, it may be death; it may be success, it may be failure; it may be happiness, it may be unhappiness.

Each moment . . . this is it.

About the Author

シ

O sho's teachings defy categorization, covering everything from the individual quest for meaning to the most urgent social and political issues facing society today. His books are not written, but transcribed from audio and video recordings of extemporaneous talks given to international audiences over a period of thirty-five years. Osho has been described by the *Sunday Times* in London as one of the "1000 Makers of the Twentieth Century" and by American author Tom Robbins as "the most dangerous man since Jesus Christ."

Osho has said about his own work that he is helping to create the conditions for the birth of a new kind of human being. He has often characterized this new human being as "Zorba the Buddha"—capable both of enjoying the earthly pleasures of a Zorba the Greek and the silent serenity of a Gautam Buddha. Running like a thread through all aspects of Osho's work is a vision that encompasses both the timeless wisdom of the East and the highest potential of Western science and technology.

Osho is also known for his revolutionary contribution to the science of inner transformation, with an approach to meditation that acknowledges the accelerated pace of contemporary life. His unique "Active Meditations" are designed to first release the accumulated stresses of body and mind, so that it is easier to experience the thought-free and relaxed state of meditation.

Osho Meditation Resort

 ৵৵

The Osho Meditation Resort is a place where people can have a direct personal experience of a new way of living with more alertness, relaxation, and fun. Located about one hundred miles southeast of Mumbai in Pune, India, the resort offers a variety of programs to the thousands of people who visit each year from more than one hundred countries around the world.

Originally developed as a summer retreat for Maharajas and wealthy British colonialists, Pune is now a thriving modern city home to a number of universities and high-tech industries. The Meditation Resort spreads over forty acres in a tree-lined suburb known as Koregaon Park. The resort campus provides accommodation for a limited number of guests, in a new "Guesthouse" and there is a plentiful variety of nearby hotels and private apartments available for stays of a few days up to several months.

All resort programs are based in the Osho vision of a qualitatively new kind of human being, who is able both to participate creatively in everyday life and to relax into silence and meditation. Most programs take place in modern, air-conditioned facilities and include a variety of individual sessions, courses, and workshops covering everything from creative arts to holistic health treatments, personal transformation and therapy, esoteric sciences, the "Zen" approach to sports and recreation, relationship issues, and significant life transitions for men and women. Individual sessions and group workshops are offered throughout the year, alongside a full daily schedule of meditations. Outdoor cafés and restaurants within the resort grounds serve both traditional Indian fare and a choice of International dishes, all made with organically grown vegetables from the resort's own farm. The campus has its own private supply of safe, filtered water.

For more information:

www.osho.com

a comprehensive Web site in several languages that includes an on-line tour of the Meditation Resort and a calendar of its course offerings, a catalog of books and tapes, a list of Osho information centers worldwide, and selections from Osho's talks.

Osho International
New York
Email: oshointernational@oshointernational.com
www.osho.com/oshointernational